This Isn't Me!

by

Sonia Grimes

Text copyright @ July 2017

Sonia Grimes

All Rights Reserved by

Sonia Grimes

Published by Satin Publishing

ISBN-13: 978-1974156306
ISBN-10: 1974156303

Author Biography

Sonia Grimes is a former professional drinker and drug taker, lost for so many precious years, but now found safe and well, and with hopefully, not too many battle scars to show for it.

I wrote this book because I had to. It was burning a hole inside me and now it is done. I feel at peace – although I am not sure my readers will! It is my first book, but not my last. It is an apology to those I love most, and my way forward with honesty and integrity.

Now a nutrition and weight loss coach with my own company; YOUtrition, I focus on using the strategies from within me that finally got me sober, and offer them to others who struggle with their food demons. I write programs and plans that work for my clients, I have published various articles on nutrition, and have my own Health & Wellness show on my local radio station.

My next book, a mix of YOUtrition's simple stress free recipes and food strategies that work so well for my clients, will be following shortly – probably on the next bus!

AUTHOR LINKS:

www.you-trition.com

https://www.facebook.com/youtritionUK/

www.instagram.com/loveyoutrition/

www.linkedin.com/in/sonia-grimes-01071964j

Publisher Links:

SatinPaperbacks:

http://www.satinpaperbacks.com

http://www.satinpublishing.co.uk

https://twitter.com/SatinPaperbacks

https://www.facebook.com/Satinpaperbacks.com

Email: nicky.fitzmaurice@satinpaperbacks.com

Acknowledgement:

In very loving memory of:

David Andrew Brundell, a gentle giant and the very best there was.

Sonia Hilda Hughes, my mother, who loved to laugh.

Bandit, a founder member of the original Gang of Three.

Dedication:

To Christopher, my son. The beat of my heart and joy of my life. Always and forever my Number One

To MN, who 'saw' me when I couldn't. My Silly Ol' Git. I love you.

Table of Contents:

Roulette

What makes one person a social drinker and another an alcoholic? How is it that some can drink for years and not become addicted, whilst others seem to freefall in a matter of months straight into the abyss of alcoholism? Can you feel the point of 'alcoholic no-return' racing towards you, or does it approach with stealth, drawing you in and then like a Venus Fly Trap, snap shut over your unsuspecting head tightening its grip as you struggle to escape?

Nearly thirty years ago, I was picked at random from the hundreds of thousands of young people who drank, to be an unwitting participant in the game of alcoholic Russian roulette. My turn came and, on the spin of the barrel, I lost and was shot in the mouth with a bullet in the form of a litre sized bottle of vodka. No matter how many self-surgeries I attempted over the years, (my futile endeavors to quit drinking), that bottle stayed firmly lodged, leaking a steady trickle of booze down my throat.

I was an addict, a victim of alcohol. It wasn't my fault, and I had no choice but to accept it.

Along with all the others who played and lost that game, alcohol became our lives and there was nothing we could do. Alcohol came first, before our families, friends, sanity, work, responsibility, everything, and whilst we fought, sometimes for our very lives, we could not win because drink had chosen us. Drink had chosen me.

I knew this to be the truth because I spent at least fifteen years fighting my addiction with no success. Yes, I had periods of abstinence, but I knew even then, while I was sober, that it wouldn't last. It was literally my daily struggle; a raging war between my willpower and addiction. Only addiction never gets tired or runs low on energy the way willpower does. It is a mighty force, that can defeat the strongest armies raised by family, intelligence, want, desire, interventions, therapies, and, what I believe to be the strongest army of all, love.

For most of the twenty-seven years that I was consuming booze, I was being consumed as well. I was sure there was no hope or chance of change or even at the end, survival. Whilst I said out loud to myself in the bathroom mirror and again at AA meetings, "My name is Sonia and I am an alcoholic", the inner me whispered back from the black bottomless pit of self-disgust that had become my constant companion, "This isn't me".

There are no words to use that could convey to you, on any level, the depths of despair that came with my finally knowing and accepting that I was an alcoholic after my beautiful son was born. A time when I was utterly desperate to be sober.

It is impossible for me to express the almost constant feelings of hopelessness, weakness, powerlessness and self-loathing, that I daily endured, when what I needed to be for him most was strong, powerful and nurturing.

It feels now as though I awoke almost every day, of every week, of every month for the best part of twenty-seven years, with a pounding headache, swollen eyes, and a parched dry mouth. Dehydrated, yet profusely sweating and unrefreshed, with little memory of the night before and absolute dread of the day ahead. And all because I drank.

Fast forward two years and I am sober, (my God, I love writing that wonderful, miraculous word). My sobriety is the single most important relationship of my life, because it is the relationship that enables me to be who I've always dreamed to be for my son. To be the person I knew I was deep inside, but never thought I could be.

I am sober, happy and positive. My sobriety is not a daily struggle, and I do not rely on my already overburdened willpower. I do not attend or need any groups, have counselling/hypnotherapy or any other intervention.

I don't miss alcohol, I don't count the days from my last drink. I never think, "I wish I could have just the one, or, maybe one day I will be able to…" alcohol simply doesn't feature in my life. I don't 'see' it in the supermarkets anymore, where before I couldn't walk past those aisles without fighting back tears of despair and being unable to speak.

An open bottle of wine in the fridge does not come into my line of vision, to me it is just another bottle with a 'use-by date', which like milk or juice, will go sour if I don't have a visitor who wants it.

I keep Champagne on the pantry floor ready to be chilled for guests, as well as Gin for my sister's visits placed carefully on the top shelf next to my homemade Muesli. I see the blue colour of that bottle every day, but not its contents.

I can happily hold glasses of wine for my friends on nights out whilst they juggle giggling with their coats and handbags, I can smell it right under my nose and I feel and think nothing more than, 'for goodness sake, how are you are so disorganized?'

I also know, without any doubt, that alcohol does not make me more fun, more confident, more relaxed, more anything.

It doesn't fill a void; it creates one.

It gives me no comfort, it does not make my day seem brighter, instead it darkens it. It makes me in literally every way, less of a person that I value and cherish.

I have not given up anything, I have simply stopped destroying myself and my loved ones. I am not the only one who is finally free of my addiction, those I love most in this world are now free too.

Believe me, sobriety rocks!

Chapter One: Let Sleeping Dogs Lie

This is my story of how I came to be an addict, first through my use of drugs and then with alcohol, it concerns my struggles to quit for over twenty years and finally my recovery.

It is about being a single mother with a beautiful young boy and the effects it had on us individually and our relationship, both whilst I was drinking and now that I am sober. It is not a stick to beat anyone with, not even myself, and nor is it a 'woe is me' exercise to excuse myself or to shift responsibility for my actions. It is simply my truth.

I will not be delving deeply into my childhood nor pulling apart past relationships, both will only be mentioned in relation to my reactions, as they are neither the reason for my drinking nor the writing of this book.

I know that whilst there have been traumatic, painful, and difficult times in my life, which I concede may have shaped my choices, there has been in everyone's – and many more people have suffered more devastating and painful experiences than mine.

My need here is to write down my experiences for myself and for my son. It is in its smallest part an explanation, for the unexplainable, but mainly, by being open and honest, I offer this to him as my apology.

****

That said I will jump directly to my 17- year- old self. A pretty girl, I was emotionally isolated and reeling from the traumatic disintegration of my parents' marriage and my home life. My mother left home, when I was 16, after many years of unhappiness. She was home one morning before I left for school, and gone when I returned.

No explanation and no forwarding address, she took my youngest sister with her and we heard nothing for over month; a month of my still very young brothers and remaining sister asking where mummy was, and I had no answer for them.

My kisses and cuddles were a very poor second best, which when added to her loss as well as living with the previous years of unpredictable vicious arguments and stony cold silences, all came together to affect me deeply.

Not for myself so much, as for the devastating effect of impotently witnessing my much younger siblings' confusion, tears, loss of security and joy. A hurt I carry with me to this day. I felt unloved and unlovable. Inside I was shy and with cripplingly low self-esteem. On the outside, I was engaging, fun, seemingly carefree and with a big personality. At that time, my inner self was carefully and securely hidden away, probably to maintain my sanity, even from me.

So, my fragile younger self met an older man and his drug habit. He didn't introduce me to his drug habit the evening we met, that slowly dawned on me and became obvious over a period of time. I guess a little like realizing that your parents-in-law don't actually like you, it's all just been a polite mask.

At 17, I had literally no experience of drugs or alcohol. I don't think we ever had strong drink at home, and I certainly don't remember ever seeing my parents drink, or come home under its influence. I could be wrong, but my perception clearly sees alcohol having had zero impact on my formative years.

When I met The Older Man (T.O.M), He was 32, handsome, articulate, funny and the best company to be around. He was fresh faced and lightly tanned, so I assumed he had spent a great deal of time outdoors.

One of my greatest pleasures is to walk. I have always enjoyed walking for miles through woods and around coast lines and TOM had the look and relaxed air of a kindred spirit. However, what I didn't know then was that his light tan and glowing health came not from the multiple benefits of outdoor exercise, but from working in a prison garden.

I'd met him one week after his release from serving four years at Her Majesty's Pleasure for drug dealing, and the healthy glow of the prison spa was still very much in evidence.

TOM was living with his mother, which maybe I should have thought something about at the time, but at 17 and still at home myself, I didn't think to question it. I met his mother in the first week simply because we went to his house before going out.

She was lovely and delighted with me; that did feel strange. I remember it quite clearly, I was a nice, friendly girl but having left school on the day I turned 16, with little education, nor a single academic qualification, and no plans for life, I was definitely no-one's dream daughter-in-law. Even then, I knew that I was unformed in every way, and I remember feeling the weight of expectation upon me that now, because of me, everything would be better. Better than what though, I had no idea.

Of course, later on I knew that because I didn't inhabit his druggie world, it was expected or maybe just vainly hoped for, that I would be a good influence on him and keep him clean. No-one told me any of this at the time and he, and his family, kept his drug abuse a secret from me for as long as possible. As a mother now, I am horrified at the level of complicit deception that went on around a young girl who clearly had no idea what was happening, but that is just the way it was.

Back to the drugs, the first drug I ever saw was heroin and with no experience at all it could have been baking powder or a fine line of washing powder newly spilt from a washing machine. Naivety at its best made me the ideal partner for a deceitful addict and his family. Three weeks into our relationship (such a fun word to describe such a dishonest and disastrous liaison), I was offered a line of cocaine.

We were in a night club and as a non-drinker I was watching with my uneducated eyes everyone metamorphosing into comatose zombies with glazed eyes and no comprehensive conversation. ' very odd,' I thought, and when I asked TOM what was going on, he told me that our group was taking cocaine and that when it hit home, they would be up dancing and laughing again and having the most amazing time and I should try it. I am sad to say that my young, reckless, 'what the hell' attitude thought to herself 'yeah, okay,' and I did. So, my first line of cocaine was put onto a piece of kitchen foil and lit from underneath. Anyone reading this with any drug experience will know that this was not cocaine, but heroin. High five that man!

As with most first-time heroin users I was horrendously sick all over the guy; there was some justice then, but the feeling of warmth, comfort and distance from all the unhappiness that followed my projectile vomiting was a revelation to me. I basked in what I felt love must feel like, protected and secure.

My thoughts drifted away from all the pain and were free to roam without bumping into the sharp, jagged corners of my mind. Serrated edges that I'd spent my days determined to avoid, knowing they would rip at my young emotional wounds. I knew that once those wounds were open, I would bleed to death, so avoidance was imperative. Just from writing those few sentences I hope to give some understanding as to my joy at finding such a safe place which regrettably came with the deathly label heroin.

To start with heroin was not an everyday indulgence, although I believe it was for him, but as I was still very naive, if someone had told me that one of our group was dozing because they were tired, I would have unquestioningly accepted the excuse, for what was in fact; a drug induced stupor.

Bit by bit though, I allowed it to overtake me and together we used every drug out there, with heroin definitely topping the leader board for me.

Over the next eighteen months, I came to know first-hand, on a steep learning curve akin to climbing Everest, all about drugs, drug users, drug dealers, drug related suicides, a drug related kidnapping, neglected children, neglected animals, deception, stealing, borrowing of money that would never be repaid, lies to family and employers, lack of self-care and self-respect, lack of food but never a lack of booze, fear, paranoia, self-denial, self-hatred, anorexia and anxiety. And I was still only 19 years old.

This was in the early 1980's, at the beginning of the public's awareness of AIDS and we, as heroin addicts, were understandably viewed with suspicion and disgust; this worked very well for me as it was the way I viewed myself. I never used needles, I always smoked this vile drug, but many who did died within the next 10 years, not of overdoses but of AIDS related illness due to the delightful habit of sharing dirty needles.

The advent of AIDS was like a natural culling process, and devastating to already broken families. Parents were forced to watch, with impotent despair, as their beloved young adult offspring, on the cusp of a life they had hoped might contain success and happy marriages with grandchildren, become hollow-eyed husks of the babies they had dearly cherished and would always remain in their eyes.

During my relationship with TOM, there was no physical abuse as such, in fact I now believe he was a good person, simply lost in his addiction; divorced from reality and too scared to try life without the false crutch of drugs.

We all lived in each other's houses, too stoned to go home, wandering from house to house depending on where the next fix was to be had. I don't remember anyone working; I can't imagine any of us being employable. I was training as a hairdresser, which was such a wrong choice for me, but as I said earlier, having left school at 16 without a single qualification, the world wasn't exactly my oyster, and I wasn't ready to grab life by the horns anyway; that wouldn't happen for another thirty years.

I know several of our crowd came from wealthy homes and their desperate parents supplied them with the money to score (buy drugs) in a vain attempt to retain some control. Some even went and bought the drugs themselves in the hope of keeping their children out of the seediest drug dens. The drugs there were, cut with goodness only knows what, were a potential and instant death sentence. So, we sat drugged up to the eyeballs watching daytime TV; I say watching, I don't remember a single thing and we may as well have been staring with glazed eyes at a cornflakes box for all we were able to absorb. When we finally roused ourselves to any extent, there was the pub, then back to our cornflake box. Wow, what a life!

I didn't know then, and probably never will know, how it was that I seemed to hold onto some semblance of reality. Maybe those two intervening years weren't quite enough to come to terms with all the shocking new experiences. I still remember a grubby small child running around a drug house with no nappy, seemingly happy and with both parents physically present, but both mentally and emotionally in another universe; totally unfit to care or feed their little boy. I can even remember his name. Possibly, because I had younger brothers who at that time wouldn't have been far different in age, who I absolutely adored, seeing that small, vulnerable child upset me terribly, so I sat and fed and played with this gorgeous little fellow until we left.

I remember calling Social Services that same day, telling them about the boy, his parents, the drugs and giving them the address. For weeks afterwards I was paralyzed with terror that I might be exposed as the one who had broken the sordid code of silence that all drug addicts live by.

This charming sham of a life continued for probably somewhere around two years. I'll be honest, they weren't two years of hell; no-one forced me and I don't remember feeling any pressure, at that point I probably didn't need any coercion anyway.

His parents blamed me for his return to drugs (although he had started taking them the day he left prison), and I think later that I blamed myself too. Such a ridiculous notion I now know and one that that his parents with all their previous experience should also have known. An addict is the only one who can save themselves and at the time, neither of us wanted saving.

Still, I knew that this so-called life we lived was wrong, dishonest and destructive and that I was very, very wrong to be a part of it. I also knew that in the circles in which we crawled, I was utterly alone in my thinking.

Nine months into the relationship I stopped eating; I don't really know why, or maybe I just can't remember. I became almost silent, the change was incredible. I was unaware of my weight dropping off and the change in my personality, but the shock hit me when I saw friends outside of our drug-fuelled twilight life; I remember sitting in a pub with some girls from school and hearing their extreme concern that I was far too thin, pale and looked terribly unwell. I was asked if I had AIDS and I didn't even have the energy or will to communicate with them, I simply just left before I fell asleep at the table.

I seemed to be in a fog, not just stoned, but wandering around without seeing anything around me, and then my hair started to fall out. I remember looking at food and not recognizing it as a thing of pleasure, but instead almost fearing it (I have no idea how my brain came to that conclusion, but I do remember the feeling). The small amount I did eat had no taste or smell and I had to literally force myself to get the food inside me, crying helplessly as I did.

I knew on some level that this couldn't go on, I couldn't go on.

I also remember so clearly the day I stopped taking heroin. I have no idea where the idea came from, or why. The few friends I still had who weren't involved in my sordid world, as well as my doctor, were constantly telling me how ill I looked and were concerned that I couldn't survive much longer.

Selfish as it sounds though, none of their concerns or pleas had any impact on my behaviour.

On the day I stopped, there was no plan in mind, no conscious thought anyway and I wasn't particularly unhappy. TOM and I had an argument and he went out to score. Because I was in such a rage I shouted something about him not bothering to save me any (heroin); I didn't want it. He didn't need telling twice, it was all the more for him, and so he came back a couple of hours later in a state of sweating, drugged up bliss. I asked where my share was and got the obvious reply that I hadn't wanted any, so he'd had it all; such a caring, sharing environment I lived in.

I went nuts, we both knew that I would go into withdrawal very soon, and panicking and crying I ran into the bathroom. Staring at myself in the mirror a miracle happened. I don't believe in any gods and don't even like the word miracle, but twice now in my life it is the only word I can use to describe what has happened, and this was one of them.

I looked at myself in the mirror and finally saw the sick, pale, shell I had become; a young girl verging on anorexia, whose hair was falling out and whose teeth were yellow from lack of cleaning, a near skeleton with the look and smell of death wrapping itself insidiously around me. I saw in my mind's eye the lovely Sister I had been, and still was under this disguise of a walking dead shadow of a person. I was a Sister who adored her siblings and loved to laugh. I saw all this in the strangest instant and said aloud, just to myself, "You stupid cow, what have you done?".

That was the last day I used heroin. I was 6.5 stone which at 5ft 8" is dangerously underweight. I was anaemic, constantly exhausted and unable to even scrape together the concentration required to drive my car.

I don't want to make it look as though walking away was easy. I did have strong feelings for TOM and, at that time, would probably have said it was love. Although now at 53, I cannot for the life of me recall exactly how I felt or even imagine where I got the strength from to both physically and mentally make the break, and not just from him, but from the drug I loved; but I did. I collected my pathetic bundle of clothes, walked out of that house and never looked back.

I went home and lay in bed for a week, shaking, sweating with terrible diarrhea, crying, hallucinating and all-in-all, in the most appalling shape of my life. I truly thought I was going to die; I felt like screaming, but didn't. I have always been able to protect my brothers and sisters from much of how I felt, and certainly when I was younger, that to me was paramount. I told my poor old Dad, already struggling under the strain of a large family without a mother, that I had tonsillitis; he thankfully was also so naïve he believed me, or maybe he didn't. Maybe he knew something of the way I had been living, although he had never mentioned it, and was just relieved that his crazy daughter was home.

After two truly hellish months, the likes of which I doubt I could ride out again, I survived the torture of my crazy brain screaming at me to go back, and looking and feeling a physical and emotional wreck, as well as suffering from malnutrition, I did what any 'intelligent' recovering addict does (although at that time I wouldn't have even known that I was in recovery), I left my home and got a job in a bar and on a daily basis surrounded myself with that other highly addictive substance, alcohol, and started again.

Of course, my old addict chums came to see me. I was offered drugs 'on the house', I was told they missed me, my sparkling wit and conversation, all of which they would have been totally unaware of as we were always 'out of it' and worst of all, I was now clean.

Being clean to other addicts is a very bad thing, it brings sharply into focus something that they absolutely do not want to see or acknowledge. If I could do it, could get clean and stay clean, then there was no excuse for them not to as well. No, it was best I came back into the fold; as we all knew, once an addict, always an addict. There's nothing great about being clean after all is there? Who needs self-respect and mental and physical health when heroin is on offer?

Thankfully there was something inside me then that was stronger, maybe it was my survival instinct or the fact I hadn't quite hit rock bottom yet, but was aware enough to see it racing up to greet me. Whatever it was, whilst my physical self was shaky at best, my mental resolve was iron clad and I told them all exactly where to go. I remember screaming like a mad woman in carparks, not caring who saw or heard, as I was stopped and offered a 'treat' by various addicts, and me just wanting them gone.

Man, I can be scary! They would scurry away terrified of the attention I was attracting, whilst being totally unaware that everyone else in the vicinity would be just as terrified at the thought of approaching this mad woman. I clearly needed no assistance, just locking up. I was exhausted, shaky, even tearful but firmly defiant and resolute in my rejection of them and their drugs.

However, whilst heroin was off the table, I continued to use and abuse a myriad of mind altering drugs on an intermittent basis for the next 10 years, 'recreationally', in my quest for peace of mind and happiness, never realizing that the peace I craved cannot ever be found in the form of any drug; be it a tablet or a bottle.

For a long period of time, I had no real friends. No one trusts a junkie, and quite rightly they shouldn't, which I understood. Even the junkies don't have real friends within their druggie circle; there is no honour amongst this type of thieves, and I had alienated everyone outside of it. I was also not in any sort of fit state to establish new friendships, although there were some lovely people who held out their kind and willing hands.

Reading the above, and to some extent reliving it, makes it even more incredible to me that my alcohol addiction lasted for so much of my life. During those long and destructive years, I would look back at, in my eyes, my astonishing recovery from this hugely addictive drug which frankly I loved. It seemed to me an incredible achievement which showed me that I had amazing willpower.

Actually though, no willpower was involved, but it took me nearly thirty years to realize that.

Chapter Two: Climbing into the Bottle...

Working in the social environment of a bar, with its late nights and after-hours lock-ins, then onto nightclubs, alcohol started to play a larger part in my life. Not a big part at first, but as I started to feel a member of the human race again, I threw myself into the world of heavy partying.

I remember going to clubs and drinking pineapple juice (bless!), and Perrier water. I think to begin with, after the heavy drug use which had shocked my system on every level, I enjoyed the feeling of being alive, aware and in control.

However there was clearly a little demon inside me that after a period of recovery, started to whisper in my ear, "Everyone drinks, it doesn't seem to hurt anyone, just have a few." So I did. And I loved it! I loved the buzz, the laughter, the ridiculous situations, the racing down motorways at 4am with music blaring out, the being thrown fully clothed into swimming pools, the attention, the sitting up all night talking rubbish but being sure that every word we uttered was profound, life changing and just had to be said. How boring we must have been. I had lovely friends who would ferry me around, make sure I got home safely and wanted nothing from me other than my infectious, joyful company. I think at that time I was close to being the real me.

For probably the next two years whilst I drank far too much; at least a bottle of wine most nights, I felt it was purely social. I was only drinking when out, and I was out every night of the week. With no alcohol at home, I never had a glass of wine whilst getting ready for a party, and never drank at work, I didn't even like the taste of most alcohols. All was good. I was no different from any of my partying friends and I was in control of drink, not drink in control of me. Looking back now, if anyone had said to me then that alcohol would become a problem for me; my friends and I would have laughed. Everyone seemed to get much more drunk than I did.

During those years I met some nice men, but no-one special. I was wary and on the whole disinterested. I didn't trust my choices and I was just having too good a time to get involved in a serious relationship. Of course that changed though, and into my happy, chaotic life came real love for the first time.

This time it was with a truly wonderful man, whose real name I am going to use for reasons I will explain later, Dave. Ten years older, he was a good, kind, loving, highly intelligent, handsome, gentle bear of a man who loved the things I loved, the outdoor life, to walk, he loved dogs the way I did, was fantastically kind and welcoming to my brothers, tolerant of my happy craziness and sometimes unpredictable moods, patient and generous of heart and spirit. And an alcoholic.

Again, the realization was slow, painfully slow this time (when will this girl learn?), and when it became impossible to ignore, I thought; 'okay, this time round I know what I am getting into and I am prepared'. I was determined not to get too attached, to not allow anyone else's standard of behaviour become mine. Instead I decided to enjoy the best and leave the rest, and at least it wasn't heroin. How foolish I was. I didn't understand at the time that addiction... was addiction... was addiction... Be it food, booze, drugs, even relationships, they all follow the same basic pattern, and all have the same devastating consequences; loss of trust, honesty, respect, friendship, family, self-worth, self-love, self-care and now I know, life itself.

Addiction is another word for loss, as there are never, ever any gains.

Dave and I had a wonderful few years together. I felt really loved, adored even and never judged. We held the same values, we laughed so much, walked all over the coastlines of England, volunteered at an animal rescue centre at the weekends, had good friends and we rarely fought; – he was so gentle and that encouraged me to be much less of a firecracker. Plus, to start with, or so I thought, he hardly drank. In fact, I would have said that at the start of our relationship, that I was the drinker. I know now that he did drink though, just never around me.

We would go out in the evening to a club, get merry and he would take me home. I was aware that he would often call me much later with a slurred voice and ramble on about absolutely nothing until I finally shut the conversation down. He could never really remember the conversation the next day but he was never aggressive when rambling, so I just thought it was funny. I now know that this was classic 'drunk dialing', something I mortifyingly did far too many times myself years later.

About a year into our relationship, his drinking; that nemesis so well hidden in those early days, but in whose grasp he was already so firmly held, started to slip insidiously more and more into both our lives. To start with we would go for a picnic by the river every sunny Sunday and take one bottle of wine with us, which would last the whole afternoon. As time went on that one bottle would last us just half an hour, so we went from one to two, to three, to vodka, to disaster. A disaster I don't even believe we walked blindly into. I think we both knew that we were drinking too much, we just didn't know why and on the whole, we were still enjoying life. Not as much though. I started to wake with headaches, tired and my joy of life seemed diminished.

In the worst of situations I have always been able to see light and laughter, now I felt there was less of me. The days seemed longer and duller. And yet I never saw a connection with how I was feeling and alcohol. I am astounded now by my lack of insight. Today it is so obvious to me and yet it wasn't back then.

I know I was really shocked the first time Dave bought a bottle of vodka for us to share. I didn't know anyone who drank vodka at home, still it was fun to sit watching TV in the evening with a vodka and orange, chatting and laughing. The first few times we would drink probably half the bottle between us, and I would be totally pissed and pass out.

My tolerance grew quickly and within months of that first bottle we were drinking a whole bottle between us most nights. We reasoned to ourselves that as we had no children or responsibilities other than our beloved dogs, our drinking affected no-one but ourselves, and probably in the beginning we were correct in that. However regular drinking on that scale quickly takes its toll, and as we started to damage ourselves, that damage reflected back into our world, upon our view of ourselves, our families, friends and employers.

I couldn't tell you for many years when the tipping point came for me; when social drinking became addiction drinking. I don't even remember when I first started to think 'I need a drink' as opposed to 'I feel like a drink', but I now believe it was around the time my mother died.

I was 27 years old when my mother was killed in a road accident. I'd had a difficult relationship with her after she left home, after I felt she had abandoned my brothers and sisters, had hurt them so badly, and yet her loss hit me unbelievably hard. It was not because of the relationship we'd had, but because of the loss of the possible relationship that our future might have held. I thought I didn't love her and I knew she didn't love me.

However, I realized on that awful day, the very moment I received that devastating telephone call, that I loved her desperately. That all her children did. Her tragic, unexpected death smashed us, like a window shattering outwards after a bomb blast. The longest sharpest shards of pain and grief were hurled at her precious, vulnerable children, slicing indiscriminately through our delicate skin and travelling with relentless precision into our young already fragile, hurt hearts. For most of us, those painful shards have stayed lodged and untended within us to this day. Our hearts have healed around those shards but still, after almost twenty five years, they can shift and twist unexpectedly and our infected wounds ooze that same painful bleeding all over again.

Back then we didn't think of grief counselling, we just 'got on with it'. There is no fault to lie at anyone's door, we just didn't have the coping skills, I don't think we had even heard of them. I know from my side at that time, whilst my arms and heart were always open to my brothers and sisters, I would never have reached out for myself for fear of causing a further dimension to their grief. I think now we all felt the same way.

On the night before her funeral, I sat in the Church with her coffin in a numbed state of disbelief, I only left when I was asked to as the priest wanted to lock up. I didn't want to leave her in case she woke up, this sounds insane now, I know.

The next day, of course, we all survived her funeral, the hardest part of which by far for me, was watching her six beautiful boys, my brothers, the youngest only 18, carrying their mother to her grave. It was their decision to do that, and one they made on the day. They had seen the pallbearers and decided, almost as one, that they wanted to 'hold her' one more time.

However, one of my brother's was so upset he didn't want to carry her, and they all agreed if one didn't want to – then none would; to protect the upset one from future regret. There was no argument, just total love and then they all agreed they would. My wonderful, perfectly imperfect brothers. That sight will never leave me and I don't want it to. It was beautiful and felt totally right.

Afterwards I tried to comfort them, but there is no comfort at such a time, no solace to be found anywhere, nothing. And so, we all retreated into our individual, internal emotional safe houses, carefully constructed and bullet proofed to repel any further pain.

That night I went home and I drank almost the whole bottle of vodka. The most I had ever drunk in one go and I think I was lucky to wake up the next morning. I felt so ashamed, so wracked with guilt at what the consequences might have been to my siblings, and now I felt so wretched, depressed and frighteningly unwell, I couldn't even lift my head from the pillow, let alone get out of bed. I couldn't open my eyes, I couldn't speak. I simply lay on the bed dry retching into a washing up bowl, crippled with grief.

For most people, having had a binge like that and the feelings of shame and unwellness that come with it, would have been enough to put them off alcohol for life. Not me. The total oblivion the alcohol had afforded me became what I craved most; not every day or even every week to start with, but I began to feel the need to lose myself completely at times, and so I did.

After my mother's death I immediately changed jobs. I wanted to be where no-one knew of my loss. I didn't want sympathy, I didn't want to be asked how I was, I didn't want kindness or support. I wanted to forget and move on, but of course, I took my grief with me everywhere. I didn't wear it, it wore me like a huge all enveloping burka, with only my eyes peeping out, and to cover those I put on sunglasses.

Her death had been just after Christmas and in the February the weather deteriorated. One day, as I was standing by the photocopier in an anonymous office, it started to snow. One of the shards of pain lodged in my heart twisted sharply and I mentally collapsed. I suddenly realized that she would never see the snow again and that I would never see her. I walked out of the office, past all the bemused staff, got in my car and drove home.

I bought a bottle of whisky and knocked most of it back in one go. I think now that I was screaming for help in the quietest way that I knew, and that hopefully, wouldn't disturb anyone else.

Dave came home hours later and thought I was dead. I had vomited whilst unconscious and thankfully had rolled onto my side in my drunken stupor. We were both sure that had saved my life.

Had either one of us been more enlightened or not an alcoholic (unaware at that time though that we were), we would have realized that I needed help urgently. However, neither of us was capable of any coherent thought processes so we did what we always did in times of stress; we had another drink.

Chapter 3: Becoming a Shell

Life moved on, and for the most part I was able to hold down unfulfilling, but all I could manage jobs, still see friends and family, and to the outside world continue to 'be Sonia'. A less bright and shiny version, but still one that was recognizable enough to stop anyone delving deeper; no questions asked meant no answers had to be given. I was like an award-winning actress, always able to be what I felt other people wanted or expected of me, whilst I had completely lost any notion of who I actually was. What I did know was that I was not good enough and that I was slowly disintegrating inside.

Every day now, I would go home, pour a large vodka with a drop of orange, and sit in the garden, regardless of the weather. I actually preferred the cold and the rain, it seemed more real to me than any other aspect of my life at the time and I would cry; emotionally and physically depleted by my day's performance.

Not one person understood my desperate inner turmoil, least of all me, and whilst I had a few good friends, any of whom would have dropped everything just to listen to me, support me and care for me, I said nothing. My escape and my closest confidante of choice became vodka. Everything suffered, except our dogs, they always came first. They were fed before we were, exercised twice a day and cared for in a way that I at least, had totally abandoned for myself.

Over the eight years Dave and I lived together, slowly but inevitably, our alcohol addiction hugged us tighter. It took over our goodness, our kindness and our loving personalities. We became unreliable, aggressive and deceitful. Our health began to suffer both physically and mentally and I slipped back into the depression that I have suffered from on and off since I was 16.

We both continued to work at jobs that demanded nothing, and got nothing from us. We didn't' have to hide anything from anyone, we didn't have to pretend and so there were no brakes on our drinking which, although we weren't aware of it at the time (and would probably have denied), was spiraling completely out of control.

I remember concerned friends trying to tell us, some of them very clearly, that we were in trouble. But I also remember telling them where to go, not to interfere and that they didn't know what they were talking about. They didn't understand and I didn't tell them that the only reason I was able to function on any level was due to the alcohol. That it kept the emotions I couldn't deal with at bay, that without it I wouldn't be able to 'be Sonia', and I definitely wouldn't be able to cope with my life. As far as I was concerned It wasn't their business anyway, and of course I planned to deal with it when I was stronger.

I believe I thought at the time that if I could overcome heroin, then alcohol would be nothing compared to that. How wrong I was, I now know that of the two, alcohol was much harder for me to deal with because it is socially acceptable (until it isn't), it is literally everywhere and that you are considered dull and a killjoy if you don't drink. The cultural view in the UK seems to be that alcohol plays a vital part in every celebration. Well my 'celebration' lasted twenty seven years and every single year of it was wasted.

As well as the physical and mental costs of regular alcohol consumption, there is the financial cost. We had chosen vodka, and to start with top quality vodka. That was all to change over time though, as our tastes became less about the palate and more about the super strength alcohol we required. So Cider joined our happy family party and vodka became an expensive indulgence as the monetary cost of our combined drinking began to take its toll.

Our uninspiring jobs and our uninspiring, and unreliable selves, meant that we were paid uninspiring salaries. We got badly behind with all our bills as well as the mortgage, and finally Dave had to borrow a substantial amount of money to get the mortgage payments back on track. Borrowing appeared to be our only option as it never entered our heads to cut down on the booze. None of our friends had much disposable income and to my eternal shame, I do not believe we ever paid the mortgage money back.

I have to write here that when I use phrases such as, 'I believe' or 'I think', I am not trying to dilute my story or offer myself a way out, it is simply that a great deal of my specific memories are alcohol soaked, so are not 100% reliable. Where I haven't written either of those two phrases, I am confident that my memory is shamefully intact.

As our drinking became literally part of our personalities, our behaviour became increasingly unpredictable and volatile. Whilst I have some amazing memories of the early days of our drinking, over time these become few and far between, as our drinking turned us into the Ugly Sisters in a pantomime that had become our life. Unpleasant to be around even to ourselves.

We would get drunk and go to parties, and once where we would have been the life and soul, we now fought, ruined everyone's evening before going home to sleep it off, blissfully unaware of the chaos and hurt we had left behind. We would always apologise when we remembered, but sorry is not just a word, it should translate into action; a change of behaviour, and our 'sorry's' quickly became hollow and unacceptable.

Why did we allow this to happen? Two fundamentally good, decent people who, when sober, were the couple everyone wanted to know, and yet when drunk, the ones everyone wanted to avoid.

Strangely, there did seem to be some boundaries, which we didn't, I like to think couldn't, breach. For instance, we never stole money directly to fund our drinking, to us borrowing and not repaying sounded much less worse, even though borrowed monies not repaid is ultimately stolen. I, in particular, had plenty of opportunities to steal, especially at work, but I could no more have taken the petty cash for example, than not feed my dogs. With so few memories from that time of which I can be proud, I am weirdly proud to be able to write that.

I remember one incident which highlights these boundaries, and thankfully it is not the only one, but one which is also a little light relief so I will share this with you.

One afternoon when we were out walking, we found a bulging purse on the pavement. We grabbed it and for a minute I am sure we both thought without saying so, 'wow, let's get drunk!'. However, when I opened the purse I found it bulging with coupons carefully cut from newspapers and magazines, as well as paper money. We didn't touch the paper money, so I have no idea how much was there, but it looked like someone with their finances very much in mind had dropped it on their way to the shops.

Quite a long way in front of us was a woman with a pushchair. We hazarded a guess that she might be the owner and ran after her, calling out about this purse. She must have been terrified to see these two-dishevelled creatures bearing down on her, particularly Dave who really did have the size and lumbering gait of a wild brown bear. Quite understandably, she took one look at us and she too started to run, and her poor young child started to cry in fright. Something very strange happened then; because of our alcohol induced paranoia, both Dave and I panicked and ran after her faster than ever before, each of us inadvertently feeding the others paranoia, thinking, 'shit! What's she running from? We'd better go with her, she can look after us'!!!

What on earth...? So, these three terrified adults, and one even more terrified child, ran full tilt into the nearest shop and Dave, with great presence of mind, barricaded the door to keep out the monster; little knowing that we were the monsters! I was crying with relief to be in the shop and sobbingly went to the woman and gave her the purse back; it was then her turn to cry with relief and thank us profusely.

The monsters before her, now shrank in front of her eyes to two kind, slightly strange but no longer menacing people, and once her fears had evaporated so did ours. What a relief! So how did we celebrate? Oh, yes, a large vodka in the pub. I write this story with a smile, as I feel in some way it shows that even during our terrible addiction, there were some glimpses of the good people I know we really were; although those glimpses were sadly rare.

Predictably, the drinking that had started out in making us laugh, that strengthened our bond and encouraged our reckless but harmless fun, turned our relationship into a co-dependent shell of what it had been. In the early days, we were a couple that stayed out dancing until 6am, then walked home along the river before a quick shower, change and off out to breakfast.

We made some crazy holiday choices, the photos of which I treasure, but the drinking had now bought our lives to a standstill. We stopped growing individually and as a couple; our lives became stagnant in every area. We no longer had any real respect for one another and little tolerance. We were angry, snappy, resentful, irritable, depressed and moody and yet, not once, did we put any of what we were feeling or our actions down to booze. Alcohol had eroded every part of us and led to ridiculous, drink-soaked arguments.

I am sure we blamed each other for the total mess we had made of our lives, and I am also sure that we stayed together because it was easier than being apart, or maybe we just couldn't be bothered to go through the process of leaving. The drink that was driving us apart was also the glue keeping us together. I knew without a shadow of a doubt, that I still loved 'the early days Dave', a Dave that I now only rarely saw, but knew without any shadow of a doubt was still there and I know he loved me, probably for the same reason. By now though it had become the most destructive relationship I have ever known. At least that was true from my side and I can no longer ask Dave.

And so began my slow and painful realization that we could not continue on together. I knew by now that the alcohol had become a serious problem, and I suspected that it would become a death sentence for both of us.

I didn't want that, I tried to climb out of the hellish pit that we had created for ourselves and to bring him with me. I wanted so badly for him to come with me.

I truly believed if we could learn to manage our drinking, not stopping completely, because I didn't want to go that far, but to substantially cut down the amount we drank, we could regain us. I had no doubts that I would die young and, as I had no children, it didn't matter to me. However, I thought if we could just reduce our drinking, it might not be so imminent. Sadly, Dave didn't share my belief. We talked about being sober and then had a drink to toast our new resolutions. It was hopeless, we were hopeless and we had to be apart.

This was the start of my forays into the various interventions available. I started going to local AA meetings and having counselling through my doctor. I knew what I wanted; to be sober(ish), happy and with Dave, but I didn't or couldn't admit that I was an alcoholic. I recognized myself in every story I heard, but still somehow thought that I was different. I started to lie, even in AA. In fact, I lied to almost everyone about my drinking in those days, and even more especially to myself. I suppose whilst I didn't really see the extent of my problems, I did know I wanted something different. Anyway, with any level of self-denial in place, no intervention can work and so it was a depressingly unrewarding experience both for myself and those who tried so willingly to help me.

After six months of AA meetings and with the perceived failure of the intervention support, I knew I had to get out. To get away from Dave. I knew that he was not to blame for my drinking, but now there was literally no other option if I wanted to survive. I couldn't pull the partial sobriety wagon for both of us alone, I couldn't drag the heavy load of our combined addiction up the hill, whilst he lay in the back amongst the hay, swigging from a vodka bottle. It just wasn't possible.

It also wasn't possible for me to grow the backbone to be straight with him and leave in the honest way he deserved. So I took the classic way out, I met someone else at work, had an unloving affair and destroyed him.

Dave never understood that the other person wasn't the reason I left, that it was the addiction I was trying to run from, and I didn't understand that you can't run from addiction; it can run much faster! You have to face it head-on and deal with it. You have to slay the alcohol dragon.

I did know that there was no one better than him as a person, and no-one worse for me as a life partner, and that went vice versa for him. We were totally destructive together and the more I tried to change us both, the more dishonest he became. vodka bottles were hidden or filled with water instead, money would mysteriously go missing, and Dave would not so mysteriously go missing for days.

He started getting fired from jobs. He hadn't wanted to drink at home, so was drinking at work instead. Finally, to cope with all the stress, especially from a drowning me who wouldn't stop screaming at him to change when he just couldn't, my lovely, kind, and gentle Dave turned in desperation, and in search of solace to drugs - hard drugs. Heroin to be exact. That was it for me. Game Over.

This however is not the end of my story with Dave. When I needed someone at what turned out to be the most vulnerable time of my life, a few years later, he was there, as much as he could be giving it his all. He never wanted to let me down.

I wish he could be here to read this book, but he cannot, because tragically Dave is no longer alive. He died from alcohol related complications three years ago. I couldn't save him, and I know I let him down. I know I ran away, and I also know that if I hadn't run, my life would have ended in the same way.

This gloriously good man died alone, waiting for his legs to be amputated due to alcohol abuse. As I write this, I am weeping for the total waste of an exceptional person, someone who no-one wanted to know at the end because of his addiction. I wish I had been by his side when he left. I wish I could have had the honour of holding his hand and kissing him goodbye. He tried so hard, he just couldn't make it. I wish he had known how special he was, how deserving of love. My only comfort now is that I often dream of his mother waiting for him with outstretched arms, our dogs leaping all over him in ecstasy, in some special place where he is young and strong and happy again.

Chapter 4: Do I Have a Problem?

Living alone after a short-lived relationship, I assumed that as with the heroin; cutting down, although not stopping drinking all together, would not be a problem. I thought that it would be much easier in fact, especially as I didn't actually want to stop. I was in for a hell of a shock; what had worked for me then, didn't work now and I just couldn't understand why.

I now started to see myself without the excuse of Dave, and it was a horrifying reality.

I found that I couldn't just shut myself away, work through any withdrawals and start again; it was an unbelievable revelation. I came to understand that alcohol is very different from drugs. It feels normal to drink every day and often it is even encouraged.

You watch on most adult TV shows, that there is always a glass of wine at the end of a busy day. Not drunk in haste by some down-and-out type character on a street corner or in a subway, but by the professional classes, the wealthy and handsome, the high achievers sitting in their beautiful homes, in their expensive clothes, cooking exquisite meals or attending glamorous parties. Even then, when they are drunk, they are still living in environments and having lives that most of us can only dream of enjoying.

Alcohol is ingrained in every celebration or commiseration. In fact, no occasion is deemed to be a celebration without it; exams passed, engagement announced, "Let's break out the Champagne". Relationship breakups, work disappointments, "Never mind, let's have a drink, it will cheer you up". Even worse though, you are viewed with suspicion of not being a fun person if you don't drink; you just don't fit in. Unless you are a designated driver, the pressure to drink can be enormous.

I remember occasions when I was trying to give up, saying things like, "I have an early start tomorrow" and being told, "Go on, just have one" and "Don't be boring". I can assure you, I was never more boring than when I was completely drunk, alternating between too loud and laughing, or morose, and tearful, even irrationally argumentative. The kinda gal you want to run from, not spend the evening with.

Wine bars and pubs are everywhere and booze can now be bought even in newsagents, motorway services (I find that incredible) and Post Offices. Drugs aren't like that, there is a social stigma attached to them and you still have to go looking for them, with drink it's just there, literally everywhere.

For me though, it was much more than that. I had become used to alcohol as my crutch, and I leaned on it heavily. I had slowly handed over responsibility for all my difficult or painful emotions to drink; I had abdicated the responsibility of dealing with life to alcohol. It was my anaesthetic against life. Unfortunately though anaesthetic doesn't just block out the pain, it also blocks out joy, excitement, and pleasure. Booze also takes away coping skills, leaving you like an emotionally vulnerable infant, something I only realized after I was sober.

For many years, my only coping strategy was alcohol, in any and every situation I either wanted to celebrate (and I would celebrate getting to work on time!), or didn't want to think about was doused in booze. Good day? Reward yourself, have a drink. Bad day? Console yourself, have a drink. Really, just have that drink.

And so it was that, I found myself aged 30, with most of my friends having gone through the heavy drinking phase and now out on the other side. They were getting married, having children, some were climbing the career ladder and even those who weren't had cut back dramatically. They talked of not being able to drink 'like that' anymore, and that Friday night's getting lashed at the pub didn't interest them. The few that were still drinking heavily were viewed with concern, and the subject of conversations along the lines of either "How can we help him/her" or "I really like her, but she is a nightmare when she's had too much to drink".

Spending the evening plastered wasn't seen as fun anymore. All the talking rubbish and then having a pounding head the next day, where no longer the badges of honour proudly worn as they had been in the 'good old days'. What on earth was going on here? I wanted to fit in, so I started to say the same things, only each pronouncement was an unmitigated lie. It is soul destroying to lie to yourself every day and be completely aware that you are doing so.

I didn't want to change, and couldn't admit it wasn't possible anyway, so I rethought my drinking strategy. I started to take vodka with me on every occasion. A quarter bottle in my bag, or if it was a small evening bag, miniature bottles which I washed out and kept for the next small bag occasion, when they would be refilled. Going out without my secret friend so close, I felt fearful and exposed. Alcohol was a form of protection to me, a lovely comforting cloak to swathe myself in and repel any part of life I didn't want to touch or acknowledge.

I would make excuses and go to the bathroom as soon as I arrived at any destination, then empty the miniature bottle in one swig before the night began. The liquid seemed to have a magical effect on my body; I felt its golden burn as it slid down my throat and could literally feel it's warming, sedative love for me flow through my veins, calming my nerves and relaxing me.

Before the drink, I would see myself in the bathroom mirror with empty, dull eyes, boring and drab. Afterwards, I would see myself sparkling, alive and ready to be witty, lovely and fun. I felt that the drink transformed me from an inadequate, insecure, fragile me into what I, or those I was with, wanted me to be. I imagined that my battered, ugly little caterpillar became a beautiful butterfly, laughing and glamorous, always the life and soul of the party.

On the nights I went out to dinner, I would make sure I ate a slice of dry bread first, just to absorb the initial impact of the alcohol, and so I started out exuberant and great company, at least for the first hour anyway, but if I hadn't eaten the alcohol would hit me like a hammer. I would be in a panic about leaving the bathroom knowing that within 10 minutes I would be exposed as drunk.

Mostly, I kept an eye on my alcohol consumption in front of people, careful not to be seen knocking back the wine, and in the early days pacing my drinking, but when alone; those brakes were off.

Sometimes I miscalculated, and sometimes I forgot to eat the bread first, then disaster was sure to happen.

I remember one evening I was going out to dinner with a nice man, and as usual before he came to pick me up, I had my own little pick-me-up, vodka. This time I was talking on the phone and instead of pouring my usual measure, the one I knew from experience would take the edge off my anxiety, but not push me into obvious drunkenness, I took without thinking my 'drinking at home alone' sized swig.

I realized immediately what I had done and spat some out onto the floor, but the rest just slid down a glorious treat. Coughing and spluttering, I looked at the half bottle in my hand and saw that most of it was gone. Oh my God! There was a knock at the door and this lovely man was standing there. I let him in, we chatted normally for about 10 minutes and I left the room seemingly sober to get my jacket; I returned seven minutes later completely drunk. We didn't go out, I wasn't capable.

I would regularly return home from a very merry night out, slightly inebriated and hyper having been on an entertaining roll, which seemed like everyone had enjoyed, including me. Time for bed? 'No, not yet,' I would always think, just one more wee drink to wind down with, and so I would start guzzling the ever-present vodka bottles stashed around my home and be completely drunk before a bedtime I would rarely remember.

Incredibly because I was so 'clever', and for that I mean read 'deceitful', many of my friends who now know of my addiction, were incredulous when I told them. Almost all of them said they had no idea, and even some had no idea I drank. Wow, I was good!

I clearly remember being at dinners with others who didn't have a problem with alcohol. I saw my friends and family sip at one glass, slowly and with enjoyment, but no urgent need, whilst I wanted to grab my glass and knock it back in one go. It didn't matter what the wine was, the colour and taste was irrelevant, the fact it was alcohol was all that mattered. I would be surreptitiously guarding the bottle of wine on the table, always jealously aware if the waiter poured more for someone else than for me. I worried how I would feel when that one bottle was empty, knowing I couldn't expose myself by suggesting another. Stress and anxiety would build up inside me, until another trip to the bathroom for another relaxing, calming, despairing, shameful, secret swig of my elixir.

I clearly remember the ever-present guilt, and depression, and the wishing desperately that I could be like them, not me. To be able to toy with a glass of wine, pick it up, and admire the colour; swirl the liquid around unconsciously and replace the glass back on the table without ever having sipped from it, as the conversation became more animated.

I longed to be that person able to leave the table with wine still resting in the bottom of the glass, untouched because I didn't feel like drinking the rest of it. The truth is, I was much more likely to make an excuse that I had left something behind and rush back to finish off any undrunk glasses of wine, regardless of who's it was.

So many times I was on the verge of begging, "How can I drink like you?" But I never did, I was too afraid that I would be told I couldn't, it was too late for me; I had gone passed that point. I feared revealing my humiliating secret and seeing the pity in the other persons eyes. And even worse I thought, I would never be able to drink in front of them again, not once they knew. I would rather have never seen the person again, than not to take another drink.

As I write this, I am exhausted by the emotions I am feeling now, and wonder why I didn't feel them then.

So the new 'sober' Sonia continued to live. I created new boundaries for my drinking, aimed at protecting myself in public as well as keeping me safely in denial about my addiction. Never in the morning, never at work, never more than three glasses of wine out, never spirits when out. These boundaries however, blew gently in the winds of my mood and became more flexible over time, although for the most part the morning one stayed in place. This alone showed me that I no longer had a drink problem; we all know that alcoholics need a drink as soon as they wake up, don't they?

I now view myself and my drinking after the age of 30, and after Dave, as a form of schizophrenia. My personality was now split firmly into three very separate compartments; the drunk me, the sober me and the real me. Strangely the sober me and the real me were not the same. The real me wasn't a drunk, the sober me was in preparation for getting drunk and the drunk was just drunk. Sounds confusing I know. I was completely aware of the distance between the three parts of myself; the who I was, who I was perceived to be when sober and the drunk.

Luckily I was not completely alone in this knowledge, I think I would have gone mad if I had been. I have two amazing girlfriends who have known, loved and supported me throughout. Apart from flash points which were warning flares to others, I managed to keep my three selves almost completely separate. I could be, and was, a great friend; kind, loyal and reliable when I was the real me, less so when I was the sober me as my focus was on the where and when of my next drink, and finally me as the unrecognizable drunk. Still that was okay, because I had created two groups of friends and I made sure they never met. They wouldn't have anything in common, not even me, as neither would have any idea as to who the totally different me was in front of them.

To try to wrest some control back, I started to 'purge'. I don't know enough about eating disorders, even though I had been anorexic once, and close to it on a number of other occasions, to use the word bulimia, but what I do I know is that these illnesses have very little, if nothing, to do with food or weight. My behavior was certainly was nothing to do with them either. I was in a huge inner turmoil and it was imperative that it stayed internal; that genie was not going to make an appearance, if I had any say in it.

But I had to have some area of my life where I was the boss, as well as being able to punish myself for, really being me; my weakness and despair. Cleansing from the inside out, and purging fitted the bill perfectly.

The relief of purging myself of those feelings; to feel that I had at least temporarily emptied out the dreadful deep anxious pit that my soul had become, became a constant in my life and stayed with me until I finally stopped drinking.

I had to do something to acknowledge my failure and this was my way, not every day, but every time the stress of the constant lying settled into the deep self-disgust that followed me everywhere.

It started with the dry retching after one of my monumental 'piss up party's for one', and fitted exactly with my view of myself; on my knees in front of the toilet, full of self-loathing and expelling vile smelling vomit. That was what I had become.

Chapter 5: Perhaps this Time

Anyway, back to the chaos. I continued to take temping jobs; easy come, easy go. No real responsibility or commitment from either side and easy to phone in sick when the hangover made it impossible to get out of bed.

I worked for some wonderful people, but I never lasted. I left them before they left me, and the pattern was depressingly similar. I would come across great in the interview; committed, interested and knowledgeable, all of which I was. I would start working, get bored, start going to the pub at lunchtimes, get drunk and leave.

Some jobs did last longer than others, the ones I had during my attempts to cut down, some of which lasted a couple of months. During those months, my self-esteem would rouse itself, take a peek over the top of the trenches, know that I couldn't cope, sigh and sink back down again. But I was not unhappy. Most of the time, far from it. I have some great memories of some amazing people, it was just that this was my life, I was used to it and I had long learnt how to accommodate life around the alcohol, never the other way around.

At 32 I met my child's father, who was basically a good and decent man. However, I am not going to dwell on our relationship. It really isn't relevant in lots of ways to my addiction, which is the point of this book. He was gone before Christopher was born and had abdicated all parental responsibility to me, (poor child). I know, and accept that whilst we are not responsible for certain situations we find ourselves in, we are responsible for how we react. I do acknowledge that his abandonment of our son has had far reaching, and very painful consequences, but as we cannot ever really know why another person acts in a certain way, it is unfair of me to try second guess him. I don't like assumptions when it comes to my own behaviour, so I don't indulge in them with others.

We met during one of my periods of relative stability, when my alcohol consumption was under control. During those periods my physical appearance quickly and dramatically improved; my hair was thicker, skin clearer, eyes brighter, and I was less bloated. On the inside there was some improvement as well, I had better concentration and focus and was generally psychologically stronger.

However, I remained fragile and afraid as I knew my ability to control my drinking wouldn't last. Not because I didn't want it to; I always did - desperately, but because some life event would come along and give me the excuse to revert to my tried, tested (and failed) coping mechanism of alcohol. I was woefully emotionally ill-equipped, however good or bad these events were. Worse still, I was still under the delusion that alcohol had the power to make my day brighter and me stronger, when in reality it shrouded the day in darkness and left me hopeless and wretched.

As I said, these episodes of sobriety were never long lived, although this time I thought with a new man in my life who didn't really drink, I might just pull it off. I write that in a blasé manner, but at the time I was honestly hopeful for a future away from drunkenness. I dreamed that my life could be different, that I would be different, that miraculously the reasons why I drank would be gone. But gone where though? This was a crazy way of thinking, as I didn't even know what the reasons were for my drinking were.

I imagined a life of truth and authenticity, the things the real me had craved for years. I could not remember the last time I had been honest with another person about my inner self, my thoughts, my hopes, my fears. By now, not one part of me had felt real for a very long time.

I didn't think about how hugely unfair it was to pin my dreams of being whole again on some poor guy who had blindly stumbled into a relationship with a woman, who had an addiction of which he knew nothing about. I didn't deliberately set out to deceive him, I think I was still in denial myself. I knew the way I drank was excessive and damaging, but I still would not, at that time, have called myself an addict. He had got involved with a woman who put on an amazing show of normality. I appeared confident, in control, fun and carefree, the exact opposite of who I was at that time. I appeared to be able to enjoy a few drinks and nothing more.

My whole self was completely different to the person I presented, but that was partly true of him too. In different ways, each of us was broken, although I was smashed to pieces by the homemade hammer I had carefully constructed over my years of abuse. He looked like the answer to all my problems and unfortunately, I lacked the insight to know that *I* was all my own problems!

We lived together for approximately six months and of course it didn't work out. It couldn't. I placed him on a pedestal that he didn't want to be on. The poor guy could only fall from it if I wasn't healed, as I had so hoped fervently I would be.

I didn't heal and so he fell. I know that we cared very much for one another, but I was too unpredictable, too damaged and lost, and along with his own issues, it just became unbearably hard. The one good thing that came from this sad relationship was Christopher. I fell pregnant, although children had never been part of my plans, how could they when my own level of self-love and self-care was at zero?

Still, I saw the pregnancy as my one golden opportunity to finally be the real me and I jumped at the chance. I knew I could do it. I knew I could be the loving mother every child needs. I knew I could redeem myself in my own eyes through motherhood and fill my beautiful baby with all the self-esteem and confidence I had never had. I would pour my soft and comforting love all over my child like the gentlest, warming shower and feel my despair wash away as he flourished and grew. I knew all this because all women are natural mothers aren't they? I now know that they are not, and that at the time, I was one of those 'not's'.

Three months into the pregnancy his father took a job abroad; we didn't see him again until Christopher was nine months old. Within three weeks of his leaving he had met another woman and had started a new life. A life of which I was completely unaware. He kept promising to come back, but never did.

I was living in a flat above a shop and already struggling. Alienated from my own family by now and with none of his family aware of our existence, life became hard very quickly. I continued to work as a temp until six weeks before my son was born, when I suddenly fell in the street and had to stop. I wasn't, thank God, drinking during the pregnancy and of all the traumas that Christopher and I suffered, at least alcohol was not part of that drama.

My brother and sister in law where with me when my boy came into the world, and I treasure that memory because apart from them, we were completely alone. There was no celebration of his birth, no flowers or loving partner to coo over him with me; just me and him. Perfect him, very imperfect me. I knew it immediately. I looked at him and felt completely overwhelmed with love and fear in equal measure.

I was terrified of getting it wrong and too scared to voice my fears. I knew I wasn't good enough and I was right. We stayed with my lovely brother and his wife for ten days and then went back to our flat. Christopher was gorgeous in every way; huge blue eyes, a lovely smile and bright blond hair. He looked like a baby duckling and I just adored him. We settled into a very shambolic routine quickly. Not shambolic because I was a mess, more that we ate and slept at the strangest times, which suited us both very well.

He was happy and so was I.

Chapter 6: Falling into Madness

The first few months passed in a blur of total exhaustion and adoration. He slept in with me, tucked under my chin. His tiny body, perfect in every way, nestled against my heart. He was my heart. I was coping, not brilliantly, but then what new first-time mother does? Especially one completely on her own. I didn't drink, I didn't want to and I didn't need to.

Slowly though something started to shift within me. I started to sleep badly and feel disorientated during the day. The night feeds became tougher for no reason and I started to dream about my mother. I wanted to see her grave, which was odd as I had only visited it once in the five years since her death. It was then that I had watched two of my brothers put her gravestone in; one they had made themselves. I had been so upset that day for them, such a sad sight, that I hadn't gone back. Now I wanted to visit. I wanted to talk to her and hear her voice again, even though it was one I barely remembered.

Strangely I ached for her to hold me and comfort me, in a way that she never had in life. I think it's a primal instinct for a new mother to crave the experience and guidance of her own mother after childbirth. Whatever it was, I wanted and missed her desperately.

My yearning for my mother became unbearable and I would wake from my dreams crying for her uncontrollably. I tried to talk to Christopher's father on the phone while he was living in China, but he had emotionally left us and was engrossed in his new life. I couldn't understand what was happening to me; I had this gorgeous little boy, I wasn't drinking and yet still, I was starting very slowly, almost imperceptibly, to drown. I knew something was wrong, but because it wasn't wrong all the time I just thought I could push on through and it would pass. I started to exercise regularly, I mixed with other mummies, I laughed and joked, and still the cold, dark water of my nightmares started to fill my mouth and nose, robbing me of my breath as I sank.

I told no-one, and the feelings I was having started to drown everything else out. The mornings were the worst, it was almost impossible for me to speak when I got up, I couldn't leave the flat, I couldn't eat. Christopher and I became thin, but I didn't see it. Thankfully Christopher loved children's TV and I would lie on the sofa with him, almost unable to move whilst he sang and chatted away happily. Around lunchtime, whatever I was feeling would start to lift, and we would go out. I would make sandwiches and a drink and we would go to the park, with its indoor play areas and swimming pool or his favourite; a walk down to the train station to wave at the trains. For an hour or two I would make a monumental attempt to be mummy. In the early days of what I now know was my illness, it was not all bad and those afternoons were still happy for him and manageable for me. I was still able to laugh at his babyish nonsense and joy. The evenings came, and he would have his bath, story and bed. A very contented little boy and I would be relieved that I had made it through another day, thankful that the fear and panic had subsided for a few hours, and yet dreading the next day when I knew they would be back with a vengeance.

One day, as I was walking with Christopher in his push chair, I bumped into Dave. It was such a relief to see him, after all that we had been through, I knew the quality of him and I think I must have just burst into tears. For the first time, I told someone how I was feeling; all my fears, anxieties and dreams.

He didn't understand at all, how could he? I sounded insane, still... he put his arms around me and I collapsed into them. I had needed that; to fall into someone's arms and rest my exhausted head on a friend's shoulder, to lean on someone who cared for me and to feel a stronger heart beating close to my weaker one. To give up the pretense that I was fine, even for five minutes, to not feel so alone.

After I had said the words aloud, I felt some small sense of relief. Dave was amazing; a true and unwavering friend when I needed one most. After that, he visited us regularly, bringing toys and treats for my lovely boy; spoiling him, taking him out, giving me a break for a few hours. He kept talking to me, trying to understand. Just being the wonderful Dave I remembered and not drinking around us.

There were never any thoughts of reconciliation, neither of us wanted that. I think ultimately, we were two people lonely from having lived a life that wasn't real, supported by a great deal of history, who still cared for each other. Dave was truly wonderful with Christopher, he loved my son and my son loved him. Still, even with his support and attempts at understanding, my feelings of drowning didn't go away. Bit by bit they got worse. I became snappy and irritable, confused and panic stricken. My heart would race, I could hear voices and a child crying; I thought I was going mad.

A friend suggested I go to the doctor, she thought I might be suffering from post-natal depression. I decided to go and the doctor confirmed that I was indeed amidst the throes of this condition, and so he prescribed for me anti-depressants and sleeping tablets.

Such a relief to have a name for what was happening to me. I expected to feel better within days. I didn't.

It seemed that suddenly my feelings of anxiety and panic twisted into something much more frightening. I started to dream about death. More specifically: my death. I would wake up paralyzed with fear and drenched in sweat. I stopped feeling as though I was on a slow boat ride to insanity and instead on a speed boat hurtling towards it. I would be shouting and crying one minute and laughing hysterically the next. I was terrified and terrifying. I went back to the doctor and told him that I wanted to lie in a hospital bed and be looked after, that I couldn't be a mum anymore and that Christopher would be better off without me. I meant all of it, especially the last part. The doctor upped my medication and sent me home.

For Christopher's safety, and I don't exactly know what I mean by this, but I knew I didn't recognize or trust myself at that time, I moved him out of my bedroom. Dave decorated the smallest bedroom for him and we filled it with toys and books. Every morning I would hear him chattering away to himself or singing along to Thomas The Tank Engine. My heart would be breaking for him. From somewhere I knew that I had to leave him for his sake, I just didn't know how. I knew he deserved a much better mother than I could be and every day now I awoke with a hollow feeling of dread. After a sleepless night, the last thing I was able to cope with was my sunny little fellow.

I would be shouting for no reason, and then crying. How upsetting for a small and tender child. No child should be left alone with such an unwell parent, and the worst part about this terrible situation, and the one that haunts me to this day, is that there was no-one to protect him from me. No-one to scoop him up, tell him it wasn't him, that mummy was unwell or tired. No-one to tell me to shut up, tell me to think of how it was affecting him, no-one to point out that the way I was behaving wasn't normal or acceptable. He just had me and I had fallen apart in front of his trusting baby eyes.

Still the medication didn't seem to make any difference and after struggling for almost a year, I gave in, I did the one thing I didn't ever want to do around my son, and I am so, so sorry Christopher. I had a drink.

I started by drinking wine in the evenings. I would wait until Christopher was in bed and have a large glass. Initially the panic, fear, despair and disconnectedness I experienced during the day would dissipate and I would feel a small but wonderful, welcome sense of relief. I would turn on the TV and watch some rubbish comedy show and laugh. My goodness I needed to laugh. The wine tasted horrible, but I had a fleeting sense of what I felt was normality. I could feel the warmth and confidence I had only ever known from alcohol flow through my veins, and I would relax.

Taking my wine upstairs with me I would sit by his bed and if he wasn't asleep, sing to him or read him more stories. He loved that time, and I knew it was only made possible because of alcohol.

To start with I kept my drinking under control... well for me under control. I knew that I had to be fit to look after Christopher at any time of day or night, but sober I wasn't capable of that. In fact, it seemed that after the first glass of wine I felt better able to cope, not less. It gave me a false sense of much needed peace. Still no-one was aware of the extent of my illness. Not even the bloody doctor.

I remember going back to him, begging for something to work and he said to me, "No-one would know there was anything wrong with you, you look great!" I was verging on anorexia again and my hair was falling out again; I can't imagine what great looked like to him!

The few people I saw knew that I had post-natal depression. Depression is an isolating illness, difficult to explain to others and difficult for the sufferer to identify. I didn't know what feelings to attribute to my illness, or to being a first-time mother, or even to being abandoned myself; I just couldn't tell you. But I could no longer hide the fact that something was very wrong and I didn't have the energy to anyway. But the extent of it? No. No-one knew of the depths of my fear or despair. If my isolation was not always physical, it was almost entirely emotionally, even from Christopher, my beautiful boy.

For so many years I had been an expert in 'being Sonia', a sad caricature of the real one. Never low, always happy, but never me. The mornings I couldn't go out, I just didn't see anyone. The afternoons, I did my best and people were kind.

Soon one large glass of wine was not enough to take the edge off my ever-present anxiety, so I had two, then three, then a bottle. Every night. Of course, alcohol is a depressant, of course it made all my symptoms worse, and of course I was less, not more able to cope. I couldn't complete a child's jigsaw puzzle let alone cope with a small child, but still I saw alcohol as the only 'medication' that worked, and still I drank.

Chapter 7: "It Will All Be Over Soon"

By the time Christopher was about 20 months old the daily struggle had become too much.

One morning after watching through the keyhole this gorgeous little piece of perfection playing with a book, and singing Old Mac Donald Had a Farm in his beautifully tuneless baby voice, I went in to his bedroom, scooped him up, nuzzled his fluffy head, and said, "Don't worry darling, it will all be over soon".

As I said it, I almost dropped him in shock. I had said aloud what the voices in my head had been whispering to me for months. 'It will all be over soon'. I knew that today was the day I was going to leave him. I knew I had to go. I couldn't bear the pain of giving him up, and knowing that he was with someone else, and I didn't trust myself not to demand him back and ruin his life too.

I kissed his beautiful head and put him on his bed, went outside and shut his door. Sobbing, I went into my room and through the fog in which I had been living and fighting against for so long, walked to my bedroom window 'do it. Jump', the voice inside me said, 'Just go, you are nothing and you never will be. Christopher will be better off without you. You are ruining his life. Go on, just do it'. I leant out as far as I could and then heard a babyish call, "Mummy, where's my Bob the Builder hat?" I pulled myself in and ran to call the doctor. I was given an emergency appointment, as by now I was seeing him every week, which was still a pointless exercise. I don't blame my doctor for not realizing the extent of my illness, as I said before, I was an expert in 'being Sonia', but I knew now that something inside me had completely broken.

This time I saw a different doctor who took one look at me and said, kindly, "I think you could do with a rest in hospital". I remember looking blankly at him whilst he made the arrangements for me to be admitted, and contacting Christopher's father (who had returned to the UK when he was nine months old, but had little contact with him), to collect him.

I don't remember leaving the surgery, going home, packing or being admitted to hospital. Weirdly, whilst I do remember packing Christopher's clothes and favourite toys and books, I don't remember his father picking him up or me kissing my beautiful boy goodbye.

And so began my first, but not my last experience in a psychiatric unit. Again, I remember little of the first weeks, I know I had the feeling of hitting rock bottom without the possibility of coming up for air. I knew that I was finally and completely submerged under the freezing, concrete walls of terrifying water that was depression, although at that time, I still did not really know I was ill. Crying tears of pain and possibly relief for seemingly hours on end, I gave in.

Maybe on some level I knew that it was over, but over in what sense I am not sure. That crying came from a part of me I had not known existed, and never want to visit again. Ripped from my son and deserving to be so, I just wanted out. Out of life. I had no resources left. I was alive in medical terms but dead in every area of my emotional self, other than the damn crying.

I was given a room of my own and placed under 24-hour observation. This meant that someone was with me all the time; my door couldn't be closed and a nurse either sat in with me whilst I cried uncontrollably or outside the open door. I remember panicking one morning and demanding that I wanted to go home, but was told very clearly that if I continued to insist, two Doctors would be called to assess me and then I would almost certainly be placed under Section S2 (this is for patients placed under section who are either in hospital against their will, a threat to their own safety or others, or deemed so unwell that they lack the ability or insight to make decisions about their treatment). I didn't know then, but fully accept now that I ticked all those boxes.

I constantly asked where Christopher was. Thank God whoever it was had the sense to keep him away. Christopher needed the break and stability much more than I needed to see him. I didn't tell anyone where I was, although Dave found out. I didn't want anyone to know, I don't know why, I think I didn't want public confirmation that I had failed the only person who needed me; the only person I loved and was responsible for, my lovely boy. It was enough that I knew.

The stress of the last few years leaked out of my every pore; I suffered crippling panic attacks five or six times a day. I remember the first one. My God, I thought I was going to die! The world seemed to rush at me, with a huge menacing presence. I wanted to run but was rooted to the spot in terror as I struggled to breathe. Bright lights burst into my brain and noises seemed magnified but yet remained unclear. My vision swam, I felt pins and needles in my arms, my heart raced and I started sweating profusely. All in the same claustrophobic moment. I started to scream in fear and was instantly medicated. Never talked to, always medicated.

I stopped eating, I stopped speaking, I couldn't read or watch TV, I just lay on my bed and sometimes sat in the hospital garden.

As the medication was dramatically increased, I did start to resurface. I started to be aware of where I was, of the other patients and strangely the weather. Instead of just asking, I became desperate to see Christopher and I felt stable enough for him to visit. I rang his father to ask him to bring him to me. A very kind nurse went out and bought sweet treats for him as I was not allowed to leave the ward yet.

When his father came, he brought with Christopher his new girlfriend Viv. She was a small Chinese woman who spoke very little English. Christopher was overjoyed to see me and I could see he and Viv had truly bonded. I could see he loved this good, kind woman. It didn't hurt me, I was just so thrilled to see him, and I was relieved and happy to see him with a normal woman who loved him too.

I wanted to see Christopher as much as possible and the hospital agreed. Viv, wonderful, generous Viv, brought him to see me every day. She took photos of me from my home and put them by his bed. She talked to him of mummy, and told him that I loved him, that mummy was poorly and together they made cards and cakes for me. Viv is family to us and I will love her until the day I die.

As I slowly improved, I was allowed out on license. Initially for an hour or two where I would walk to the local shops, have a coffee, read the paper and return; shaky, but safe and proud of my small forays back into life. Then, finally for a weekend. It was a disaster. Fragile and afraid and still very unwell, Christopher and I went back to the flat alone.

As I looked around me, the memories of the last awful, sad morning flooded back to me in a tidal wave that left me breathless. It was a huge struggle to appear normal in front of my son. I wanted to run back to the hospital and safety, but I didn't. I was scared to show my weakness in case it affected Christopher's visits and I was determined to be his mummy at home again.

Already living a lie, I was already back to 'being Sonia'. This weekend was so important to me, I had planned to bake with him, watch some TV and help him build – he loved building blocks. We did all of those things, and when we went to the shops to buy dinner I bought half a bottle of vodka. Same old me.

After he went to bed, I had a deep 'restorative' drink of neat vodka, and turned on the TV. A panic attack engulfed me, no doubt brought on by the mix of strong medication, anxiety at being home and mainly the vodka. It was a monstrous feeling that felt life threatening. Trying not to scream, and desperate not to scare him, I tried desperately to keep the terror inside me that shrieked to be expressed.

I went into the kitchen, chose the sharpest knife I could find and drew it slowly across my arm, over and over again. Not deep cuts, not suicidal cuts, but cuts that have left scars to this day, and that somehow made me feel in control. Miraculously the panic attack subsided. Now I had two coping mechanisms; alcohol and self-harm.

Exhausted I went to bed and slept well. In the morning Christopher got into bed with me for a delicious snuggle and saw my poor ravaged arm. "Oh Mummy, all broken". Broken. Never had a truer word been spoken. I hated myself all over again.

Dave came when I called him and took Christopher out for a lovely day whilst I cleaned up, called the hospital, told them what had happened and went back in that night, and so a pattern was set; drink, panic attack, self-harm, self-loathing. Not once did I see that booze was the trigger. I still thought it was the only answer.

When I finally left hospital, Christopher came home with Viv. I was still very fragile and my confidence was shot to pieces. I hadn't been back overnight since that terrible weekend and now I walked around the flat scared. Terrified of what had happened and scared of it coming back. Kind, non-judgmental Viv and Dave were quietly there for me, for us. Not always physically, because I couldn't cope with anyone around me all the time, but always at the end of the phone. They saved my life.

I continued to take the huge amount of medication now prescribed to me and little by little started to feel more able to cope. The mornings were still tough, but manageable, the afternoons and evenings were peaceful and to start with I wasn't drinking.

As I remember that poor sick woman and her perfect, but traumatised little boy, I wish I could go back, and put my strong arms around them. To hold them tight, and give them my strength, to gently kiss their precious faces and tell them, "All this will pass. You will both be well and happy. You will walk by the river on a Sunday laughing until you cry, pretending to push each other in. You will be strong and steadfast. You will have a life of peace and happiness. Christopher, you will have the mother you deserve; a mother who is constant, a warrior for you, an anchor in the sometimes- turbulent sea of life. The safe haven you deserve. You will know that you were always loved and that you were then and always will be her Number One. Sonia, you will be the mother you long to be, the person you were born to be, the real you. You will look into the bathroom mirror every day and be proud of who you see. Self-respect will be yours. You will love and be loved. You two are the best there is out there. I know it and so will you. I promise you".

Chapter 8: Baby Steps

Life continued on, baby steps for both of us. Mine probably even more tentative and unsteady than his. I found him a nursery where he was happy and we would walk there through the woods three times a week singing.

I made sure in the mornings before he went, I was what he needed me to be, and also in the afternoons when I picked him up. During nursery time, I would do the little I was capable of, the shopping and cleaning and then collapse on the bed, refilling my almost empty tank of emotional and physical energy in readiness to collect him at the end of his day.

He would chatter on about his day for a couple of hours, proudly bringing me cards and paintings that he had made, I still have them all. Until it was his bedtime and I could relax, his day over; no stress, no trauma, no mad weeping mum. I remember this as a happy time, a place we had found a rhythm to live by.

I stored up my energy for the weekends when we would go swimming, play on the pool slides and then go to the Kids Club at the Cinema. I have the happiest memories of teaching him to swim and jumping at me into the pool, whooping with delight and screaming "Geronimo".

At the Cinema, I would have drinks and treats for him bought from home and wrapped in sparkly Thomas the Tank Engine party bags, he would swing his little legs in excitement as we settled down to the movie, and I would fall asleep.

We went to the parks and to the local animal farm with its baby rabbits, goats and piglets. There were sandpits, tractor rides and we shared our picnic. Nothing demanding in our days, just little treats, that were happy and fun.

We didn't really interact with anyone, other than Dave and Viv. I could cope with our outings, they literally nourished my soul. Then there was the pleasure of having friends over for an occasional coffee, but often I was just too shattered with tiredness, still heavily medicated and still under the exhausting illusion that I had to be someone else, someone that I wasn't, for me to be acceptable and wanted.

This worked reasonably well for about nine months. I can't say I didn't think about drinking, I did. I missed it and I saw it everywhere, but on the whole, I managed to stay away. It seems, when I look back, that when I was any version of 'being well', I did understand on some level that alcohol made things worse.

I had accepted that I couldn't stop drinking, even when I wanted to. The evidence of that was in every memory of my numerous attempts, but that I absolutely had to cut down. When life became too much though I literally had no other coping mechanism. Nothing else worked, certainly not quickly enough, and alcohol became a falsely loving parent, partner and protector from any emotionally difficult situation. I have always been a practical person, so practical challenges I met head on. I guess my years of drinking had washed away in a tidal wave of vodka and wine any true emotional growth. Alcohol is famous for stunting insight, awareness and growth.

Anyway, my focus was on limiting the damage of my depression to myself and my son, and for a time, my demons seemed at bay, not gone, but restlessly sleeping. However, as the months passed, the more restless their sleep became. I don't know if I became tolerant to the medication, or the fact that I had no other treatment or therapy to support me, or if indeed it was just that I was living again under the strain of a false life, back to 'being Sonia', but as my demons roused themselves from their uneasy slumber, the symptoms, slowly, almost imperceptibly, started to return. Anxiety started to gnaw at me once again, and panic tugged at my peace. I became scared. I knew I couldn't go back to that terrifying place. I didn't want to leave Christopher this time, I wanted to stay. Although I am a committed atheist, I started to pray, "Please God, don't let this happen". My prayers went unanswered.

This time though, I was ready and armed before that final leap into the black, out of control spiral into madness. I knew what had worked and it hadn't been the antidepressants. They hadn't helped last time (or so I thought), but alcohol had immediately. I started to drink again; same old pattern, one glass to take the edge of the anxiety off which became two, which became a bottle. Every night. Predictably the symptoms increased with my alcohol consumption. Why couldn't I see the connection? Anyway, the more anxious and panicky I became, the more the despair started to overwhelm me, so the more I drank and so the cycle started again; drink, panic attack, self-harm, self-loathing and no insight.

This time the doctor halted my decline quickly and I was back in hospital. I had failed. Everything I thought about myself was true. My son was gone again and this time Social Services were informed, I think by my doctor.

'For God's sake woman, what is wrong with you?' The medication was upped, I must have been rattling. The sleeping tablets were so powerful I wasn't fully awake until the afternoon, which was great when I was in hospital, but totally unrealistic as a single mother alone.

This time I told them about the drinking, not because I saw any connection, but simply because I was asked and didn't have the energy to lie. I was asked if I wanted any help with the alcohol, and I said yes, because I could see from their hopeful expressions it was the right answer. I would have done and said anything to get me home, to have Christopher back. Everyone relaxed and smiled at me so I knew I had said what they needed to hear. It was the last I heard on the subject and I certainly wasn't going to mention it again.

I remember much more about this hospital stay, some of it I even laugh about now. I was asked to attend a therapy session, I have no idea what the therapy was, but about ten of us sat in a circle with two psychiatric nurses and we were asked to turn to the person next to us and pay them a compliment which they were to believe and accept. Oh my God, this was a terrible mistake on their part. I turned to the poor woman next to me with a small smile, ready to say something genuine and nice. I love paying compliments so I thought this would be easy.

However, I locked eyes with her and was shocked to see me staring back. The woman had the same eyes that I saw in the mirror every day of my illness, they were exhausted, afraid, lonely and deeply sad. I was staring at myself. I couldn't speak. She became uncomfortable with my stare and I couldn't look away. One of the nurses prompted me kindly, about something I could compliment her on, and I just shook my head every time.

The poor woman started to cry and said, "Don't you like anything about me?", my answer was an immediate, spontaneous and broken, "No". It wasn't her of course I couldn't compliment, it was because I would have been complimenting me; the useless mother, the drunk. We both burst into tears at the same time and ran from the room in opposite directions. Quite understandably, I was not invited to participate again.

After three weeks, with this huge number of pills, I was on a more or less even keel again and was discharged. Now there was a Care Plan in place, for Christopher and myself. I was pleased on most levels. Christopher needed support much more than I did, and we now had regular contact with some wonderfully supportive woman who would come to our home, kindly check him out, talk to me and I did feel much better. The downside of this though, was that I understood very clearly that I had to hide my drinking. Why did no-one seem to understand that it was the alcohol not the pills that were making me better, it was absolutely the wine? So, began the biggest most destructive deception of my life. One that would last fifteen years, that would almost kill me, and one that would, at times, rob my son of the mother he wanted and deserved.

Not long after I came home the second time from hospital, I became aware that Dave was drinking heavily again. He was never drunk in front of me, but all the hallmarks were there. Constantly sucking on mints to hide his breath, always going out to the car and coming back glassy eyed, more irritable and unpredictable. He was still wonderful with Christopher but in a slightly manic way. I had seen it all before and I recognized his actions in my own behaviour.

One day I came back from the shops to hear Christopher crying and I ran into the flat. Dave was out cold on the floor and Christopher had covered him with his Thomas the Tank Engine magazine trying to wake him. I was furious (talk about the pot calling the kettle black!); I woke him and told him to go.

He was still welcome anytime, but not if he had been drinking, and I told him I would never leave

Christopher on his own with him again, which I didn't. After that, and over the next six months we saw less and less of him, until we saw nothing. He was back to drinking a bottle of brandy a day and there was nothing I could do. I could barely look after the two of us and Christopher's wellbeing was paramount. Still we missed him and I grieve to this day for his loss.

Chapter 9: A Grand Master of Deception

Our lives continued in a fairly stable manner. There certainly was no outward show of anything amiss. Christopher was happy and I, armed with strategies to avoid my drinking being detected seemed to thrive, and on some levels, I believe I really did. This time there were no warning flares to others. I was now a Grand Master in the art of alcohol deception; I learn quickly and I never forget.

For the next eighteen months, my drinking felt manageable, it was constant but within the boundaries I had set myself. I was voluntarily attending the psychiatric unit as an outpatient two or three times a week. I was offered different therapies, such as assertiveness and anger management classes which were hugely beneficial as well as some creative classes which I didn't really engage in. I felt that being creative would somehow expose the real me.

I was still drinking at this stage, probably half a bottle to a bottle of wine a night, but not knocking it back desperately in search of my immediate junkie-like hit. I was after a slower shift in perception where I was a in a place of comfort and relaxation, drinking at a more measured pace that still had the end result of a temporary release from stress, but without the debilitating hangover that would envelop me for most of the next day. That kind of behavior would have resulted in either my non-attendance at my outpatient appointments or Christopher's at nursery, both of which would have drawn immediate attention and questions would have been asked.

Probably because I was more measured in my drinking, and definitely because of the support I was now receiving, the worst of my symptoms were finally under control. I had learned how to deal with the huge, dark and threatening mountains that were my panic attacks. I remember one starting to sweep over me in the changing room of a clothes shop and me staring at myself wild-eyed with fear in the mirror. The terror of being exposed in a public place and the possibility of me running screaming and half-naked from the shop hit me. This time I started to breathe deeply as I had practiced at the hospital, instead of the ragged, shallow gasps for breath that made the attacks so much worse and 'talked myself down'. It worked! The attack came, but with no menacing power.

I sank down onto the floor shaky, and tearful and stayed there for a good ten minutes hugging myself for comfort, at the same time stunned with almost disbelief that whilst it had come, it had been massively diluted, and I had taken some of its power away. I knew then that I could do it again.

It took many more attacks to completely regain control, and for years afterwards I lived in fear of their return. Still, after that triumph (and that is exactly what it was to me: a massive, trumpet blasting triumph), the self-harming stopped. My regularly bloodied arms were no longer a constant reminder of the despairing war raging inside me and the tiny fragile shoots of a version of self-respect started to appear. Still though I thought of alcohol as the answer, and still I continued to drink.

Around the time that Christopher had started school, Viv moved back to China. She had waited until I was strong; this amazing woman. We were sad to see her go but in some ways, we all needed to move on. Her relationship with my son's father had ended. He had moved abroad again whilst I was in hospital the second time to start another new life, and although he continued to visit England regularly, he hid that fact from us and didn't contact Christopher for the next six years. With the end of their relationship, Viv pined to go home and after the death of her father, was needed in Taiwan to run the family business. We remain in loving contact to this day.

So, jogging along at our own pace, the one thing I didn't expect happened, I met a man. The first I had been interested in for a long time. Still fragile and medicated, but starting to enjoy life and making friends again, this mildly eccentric, academic man, shorter in stature but huge as a person wandered into my life. I know that to him I would have appeared to be carefree and happy. Remember, I am an expert in 'being Sonia'.

He lived next door to us and would have heard me singing and laughing with Christopher and probably thought, 'how lovely'. He wouldn't have realised that the singing in the evening was to the accompaniment of a bottle of wine, or that the laughter the next morning was the alcohol induced anxiety that I would try to hide with humour. Don't you just feel for him already? Bit by bit we became closer.

Being eccentric himself meant that most of my slightly strange behaviour passed him by. His normal is very un-normal to most! He was intelligent, funny, off-the-wall and a great Dad to his boys. I watched them interact and I knew that this was the sort of relationship I wanted with my son. Suddenly I had a role model, a benchmark for parenthood. Not all of it, of course. As I said he is odd, but they shared a normal, healthy, loving relationship and that was definitely for me. Only problem was, he didn't drink and hated all drink.

Well, I did drink and it had saved my sanity when the medication hadn't, so there was no way I was going to stop. Gone were the days of wild binges that left me paranoid and unable to raise my head from the pillow (although they would occasionally visit for a weekend). Now I would drink my bottle of wine every night, relax, fall asleep and okay, I woke up the next morning feeling wretched, with a dry mouth, sore head, unrefreshed and unprepared for the mornings, but I was fine by the afternoons, and it had made me feel a whole lot better for a while; so there was no problem, was there?

There has been no-one in my life who has tried so hard to constructively help me as this slightly odd man. Maybe no-one who has made as many mistakes and misjudgments in their help, but still no-one who attempted to put my wellbeing first; to try to heal me. He wasn't so much a knight in shining armour riding in on his white charger, but more of a man in a cardboard box riding in on a piglet. But still... ride in he did.

So, another poor guy. Neither of us understood me; my moods, my big personality, my tiny ego, my destructive nature towards myself and my loving nature towards my son, my deception or my honesty. He was the first person to take on the booze battle – a battle, which of course, he couldn't win.

His knowledge of alcohol, addiction and the lies that were intrinsic to it was zero. He couldn't understand as he watched from an objective viewpoint, the disintegration of myself on every level, when I drank, or even why on earth I would continue to pour, what to my emotionally fragile self was wretched poison, down my throat on a regular basis.

At the beginning, he had no idea how regular that basis was. It was incredible to him that I couldn't see the direct route, no stops, no diversions. Simply straight from the stable sober me to the train crash I was when drunk. The fact that I was alone with a lovely young boy made it more mind blowing to him (as it does to me now). He struggled to equate the fleeting me that he saw during the day; the laughing chatterbox, with the sad, depressed woman at the end of an evening.

I am not sure that had I not been so vulnerable, that our relationship would have lasted. The me now would never have tolerated what felt like his bullying then, but of course the bullying wouldn't have happened had I been the person I am now.

Such a mess I made and all because I drank.

Chapter 10: Why Did I Do It?

I often ask myself, why did I continue to drink? After everything I had been through, after everything I had put my son through.

What did I think about alcohol at that time? When I look back now, my drinking resembles an incomprehensible form of madness. I had to have booze. If I wasn't drinking it, I had to have a stash in the house for emergencies, but what emergency could I possibly have that alcohol would make better?

I switched back to vodka thinking that no-one could smell it. Did I really think you have to be able to smell alcohol to know someone has been drinking, that it was the only give away? What about my slurred voice, my stumbling walk, lack of co-ordination, snappy irritable overreactions and mood swings? Why did I cling, remaining completely convinced, to the lie that it 'helped' me in any way? I now cannot think of one good thing that came from my drinking. Not one.

Had it made me feel better? No. Had I relaxed more? No. Was I more fun? No. More confident? No. Did I sleep better? No! All this and that's before I even touch on the effect that my drinking, as a mother, would have had on Christopher... and yet I couldn't stop.

I couldn't see past my life without a drink, even though it would become my dream to be sober; literally what I wanted most in the world. I have read so many personal stories where people would say they were in denial about their drinking. However, I am positive that from at least my second enforced hospital stay, that I knew without a shadow of a doubt; that I was an alcoholic.

I don't think I ever lied to myself again after that time. I couldn't. It could be the only reason why I had this gorgeous child and still drank. I was vaguely aware some nights that if he woke up and needed urgent help that I would, at best, have to call someone else for assistance or, shamefully far worse, sleep through the crisis. I still didn't want, or maybe couldn't, see the connection between alcohol and my behaviour, the anxiety, depression or mood swings, but I do know that I now used the word alcoholic to describe myself, even if only to myself. No excuses there then.

I remember often looking at my lovely young Christopher and crying inside. I remember thinking that I would give my eyesight not to be a drunk. I would have breathed in his skin, caressed his little face, imprinted him on my memory and then willingly given up my eyes. A physically disabled mother would have been better for him than the emotionally unavailable and unpredictable one he had.

I often wonder what I have done to his self-esteem, his view of himself and his place in the world. I wonder if he felt loved and protected? Was home a place of warmth and comfort for him to run to, or a cold, unwelcoming shell? Did he feel confident and strong, or did he feel as though he was walking on sands that shifted and sunk between his young toes, leaving him feeling unsteady and unsure, depending on my mood?

I wonder what he thinks he deserves in life, how his future relationships will be affected. I pray he doesn't blame himself in the way children do for their parent's unhappiness. Did he feel in any way responsible for me, for making me happy? Finally, and worst of all, does this glorious, wonderful young man think he is the reason I drank?

I know most of the answers to these questions now and having gained his permission, I will talk about them later in this book.

Still as a young boy, Christopher seemed mostly to be happy and content. I tried to drink less on Friday and Saturday nights so as not to spoil his weekend. I always planned outings and in the summers, I regularly took him and a little friend to the beach. Such happy times. I would wake early on a Sunday morning, check the weather report and call one of his friend's mother's, scoop the boys up (never more than him and one other, two was all I could cope with),I'd put them in the car with a picnic, blankets, warm clothes for the drive home, boogie boards, buckets and spades and drive us down to Brighton.

We would be on the beach by nine in the morning and they would be in the freezing sea until midday. Picnic eaten, play on the beach, run around to warm them up and then two sleepy heads back in the car by four in the afternoon. Friend dropped off, home by 6pm showered and in front of the TV for a snuggle under the blanket with me; happy, tired and contented. Then the vodka would be opened, a huge shot with a drop of orange, just the one. Until he was in bed and then I would down the rest of my daily quarter bottle, minus the orange.

There were of course the bad times too. The times when I was tired, hungover and snappy. I would shout for no good reason, frustrated and impatient. Times when I was unable to concentrate when he wanted to talk to me, and intolerant if he was slow. My poor little boy.

Back to my new relationship. We all need a little light relief. My new man and I, who I will call MN, slowly became closer and more involved in each other's lives. In the early days, and before he realized the extent of my addiction, or that I was even an addict, he put my unpredictable moods and tiredness down to the pills I was taking. He didn't understand depression or mental health problems and thought I should just snap out of it. If only it could have been that easy. Still I was definitely improving, the support from the hospital was hugely beneficial, I was in a good place on the whole with Christopher and I was managing my drinking reasonably well.

There were times when the alcohol boundaries I had set for myself mysteriously fell over and I ran free with my vodka bottle, but they were rare and usually more of a misjudgment on my part than deliberate. By now I was used to the morning after headaches, tiredness and dehydration. You know the saying, no pain, no gain? Well, drinking is a package deal and I just had to put up with them if I wanted to drink. Those rubbish next mornings were now so much my normal that on the odd occasion when I didn't drink the night before, I was overwhelmed with inexplicable feelings of wellbeing the next day.

Strangely I still didn't associate either the good or bad mornings with alcohol.

Then when Christopher was 7 years old, I stopped all the medication and the outpatients. I had been on anti-depressants for so many years and I decided enough was enough. I wanted to walk by myself. Against my psychiatrist's advice, I cut down on the dosage and then over the next few months stopped completely.

After a shaky start, more because I was afraid of becoming unwell again, although I now felt stronger and free. I was proud of myself and kept busy both physically and mentally. MN is a writer and I started researching articles and books for him as well as preparing speeches for his book tours. Small shoots of self-esteem sprouted tentatively. Christopher was doing fairly well at school and all in all, life seemed to me to be on my version of an even keel. An even keel that still included vodka of course – I did say it was my version.

To MN though, regular drinking played no part in any form of a happy, well life. I have often said to him, and still say now when I am easily sober, that he has as much of a problem with alcohol as I did, but in reverse.

MN tries to control what is drunk by those around him, not out of any sort of meanness and nothing to do with cost in monetary terms, more that he sees it as poison to the body; a direct link with many illnesses and a source of arguments and destructive behaviour. I understand the way he thinks, and I don't blame after having to deal with me, but honestly, he has to learn that you can't impose your views on others. I write this not to pick at him, but to show how we arrived at the stressful situation we found ourselves in. More him than me, as he never gave up expending a mountain of energy fighting my demon, whilst I just appeared to ignore him and get drunk.

Alcohol felt like the most real relationship in my life. I didn't like it, but I knew it. I understood it, I knew what to expect when I drank. I felt safe in my very uncomfortable comfort zone, even though it made my life and those who I loved most unsafe. Alcohol to me was the ultimate 'frenemy', my best friend and worst enemy. Like a family member that you don't really like and would love not to see, there is an invisible umbilical cord that binds you together, one that is stronger than any physical rope, and so I was bound to alcohol.

Poor MN. In many ways, we are well suited. We both love to laugh and have many interests in common. I love his intellect, I find his ideas fascinating, infuriating and insulting in almost equal measure. He is never boring. And I loved helping him with his work, he made me feel I had something worthwhile to contribute, so overall, it was a good time for all of us.

He is a strong personality and a good kind heart and was so generous with Christopher and me. He eased our lives in so many ways. He took care of us, protected us, fought for us, loved us. He helped us move into a lovely little house after I told him that I dreamed of having a garden for Christopher. Then my son had his own dream fulfilled of having a puppy. We bought a gorgeous little Pomeranian we called Bandit, the day we moved in to our new home. Christopher was beside himself with joy and Bandit was his closest companion during his childhood.

We started our Sunday walk tradition. I would drive to somewhere along the Thames and then The Gang of Three; Christopher, Bandit and myself would have a long walk and, if it was sunny, a play in the river, followed by either a picnic or Sunday lunch, always followed by a huge gooey dessert, in a village pub before returning home tired and very happy. We did this rain or shine. MN turned the garage into a playroom for him, designed especially around his passions of building and computers. There were holidays in the sun and snow, his boys treated him like their little brother. As a family, they couldn't have been more welcoming. We were now part of something much bigger.

Wouldn't you think that by now, with all the care and support I was enveloped in that I could have finally stopped drinking? What possible reason could there be for me to continue? I didn't know and I couldn't stop.

To start with when we went to dinner, MN would get a bottle of wine between us and he would drink just one glass. How fabulous for me! However, he quickly realized that unlike him, I wouldn't have a few glasses then leave the rest, I would drain every last drop. I had sent a warning flare to light up the sky. He then started ordering half bottles – who on earth drinks a half bottle of wine at dinner for two? No-one I want to be with. Never mind, I adapted.

I started having a neat vodka before I left the house and taking miniatures with me. I could go to my local corner shop and pretend that I was buying them to make a cake. Obviously, those who really are making a cake with vodka in, and I can't imagine there are many as I have never heard of one, wouldn't feel the need to go through the performance I did of letting the whole shop know about this mythical cake. I would take them home, and pop them in my bag in preparation for the evening.

If I was carrying the car keys for MN, I would throw the empties in the restaurant bathroom bin to avoid detection. However, if he wasn't likely to go through my bag, I would take them home, rinse them out and refill from my secret vodka stash. When MN came to spend an evening, the vodka bottles would quickly be hidden away out of the fridge and into random cupboards; under the bed, under the sink in the bathrooms, anywhere he was unlikely to be looking for his glasses or the TV remote control. Same with the tell-tale glass with its ice and a slice.

Now when I bought vodka, I stopped putting it in the kitchen and immediately hid it in the airing cupboard upstairs, amongst the towels, then made excuses to go to the bathroom for a sneaky swig, sometimes even in the middle of a conversation.

Whilst I write in a jokey manner, I am actually very ashamed of my behaviour around MN. He had some tough times with me. He would start the evening with a laughing, happy woman and end up with an argumentative bitch. Heaven help him if he tried to ask if I had been drinking. I would become explosively abusive to a man who couldn't have done more for me and would do anything to make me happy. He used to say that I had so much anger in me and that I took it all out on him. The reality was that I was just plain drunk. Drunk then defensive and aggressive.

I would wake up the next morning feeling wretched and upset. Tearful and apologetic and always he would come around. Sometimes after a bad flare up, and he gave as good as he got, although of course he should never have been on the receiving end of the 'got' in the first place, it would take a day or two for him to calm down, but he always came back and he would always tell me he loved me, talk about how the drink changed me and how sad it made him for both of us.

As this awful crap went on at my house, Christopher sometimes heard us. I remember him saying once to me, "Why do you shout at him Mummy? He loves you". I probably made up some rubbish that put the blame firmly on MN, and of course Christopher would have believed me.

I don't know how I didn't blow this relationship; I was a complex mix of good, kind, funny, thoughtful, moody, depressed and aggressive. I don't like admitting this, but it was at times a very abusive relationship from my side.

The thing with MN is that he really did see me. He saw past all the years of accumulated self-inflicted damage and abuse. I think that was part of the reason I was so angry towards him, because he could see me, the real me, and he loved this me. I didn't know how to cope with that. I guess I didn't believe it was real, that it would last. I felt that I had to live up to this dream he had of me, the one he saw, but I knew I wouldn't be able to do it. My experiences so far had taught me that the real me didn't stay long. She arrived a very welcome guest, but something always happened and she left again quickly and the version of her I didn't like, the drinker, the depressed, confused, out of control me, the one that I hated but knew so well, took her place, like a big fat cuckoo.

My drinking became a war between MN and me. Not all the time, but there was often an undercurrent of distrust on his side. He could not understand, knowing how much he hated it, how much it changed me and how depressed it made me that I didn't just stop. I didn't know either. I couldn't explain it, I could only repeat my hollow apologies and promises, but I just couldn't stop drinking.

Chapter 11: Back on the Race Track to Rock Bottom

Christopher also began to be aware that alcohol played a part in my moods, and our life. I honestly didn't think he knew. I don't think I was even in denial about that, I just thought he didn't know. I attended every school event, always early, always in the front row, dressed so that he would be proud of me, waving and smiling, bursting with pride and love. All by myself, but that didn't matter, I have the personality of a huge Irish family so it felt like there was 10 of me cheering him on. Every sports day in the Mother's Race, every pantomime.

Christopher has dyslexia, so school was a struggle and I was absolutely on the ball, making sure he got all the help and support he needed, doing all the research myself. Never taking no for an answer, always bang on the mark. I made sure he had friends to visit and that he went to their homes. I was always happy to ferry other children around. I mixed with other mums to make sure he was included in outings and he has always had a small group of amazingly loyal friends, whose mothers have been the same to me.

In some ways, I was a good mother, sadly not necessarily in the ways he needed most. I was definitely unpredictable which must have made for a very insecure environment.

I remember him saying to me once when he was nine, on our way to a party, "You won't drink too much tonight, will you Mummy?" That was the first time he had mentioned my drinking and it stopped me cold in my tracks. If it was the first time he had said it out loud, he must have thought it for a long time, it must have been bothering him.

I was mortified, ashamed and embarrassed and said, "No darling, I won't". And I didn't plan to, in fact I took the car to make sure I couldn't. I never went out, drank and then drove home, but of course, I did drink. Good old Sonia, the life and soul of the party, was asked to stay the night so that I could have a drink, and of course I did.

Christopher is a shyer person than I am, we laugh and say that he is a cat and I am a dog. Cats are reserved, they have the intelligence to suss out a person or a situation before they make any decisions, before they commit. Dogs have no reserve, they run around madly wagging their tails and barking their heads off. Everyone and everything is their favourite thing. This sums both of our personalities up perfectly. When I am sober, I am a lovely, happy puppy, but when I am drunk I can become an unpredictable Rottweiler. Even sober

Christopher struggles at times to cope with me, he didn't stand a chance when I'd downed a few vodkas.

It was about this time that I knew, absolutely knew, that I had to do something. Now it was imperative. Christopher's awareness was the wake-up call I needed. I wanted him to be proud of me, to be able to trust and rely on me. I was genuinely ashamed and filled with remorse.

So, with my new found resolve and absolute determination I started AA meetings again. MN and Christopher were over the moon. I told MN straight that I knew I had a drinking problem. He was the first person, other than myself that I had acknowledged it to. He was delighted and relieved by my honesty, and so was I. If I was acknowledging the problem aloud, I was taking the very first step to change.

Christopher, I told differently. I told him that I felt I probably had been drinking too much, that I didn't know why, but that I didn't want to anymore and that I had decided to go and talk to others who felt the same way, so that we could help each other. He didn't really say anything at the time, but when I left for the meeting said, "You will be the most beautiful Mummy at your drinking meeting". I hugged that boy so tight, my precious son.

I went, all armed with good intentions. I listened to the talk, I was happy to say, "My name is Sonia and I am an alcoholic" and I was absolutely determined. I went three times a week, was given masses of support at home, everyone was on board cheering me on, and I didn't drink for nine whole, long wonderful weeks. I was so proud of myself. I had done it! I had kicked the habit. It was hard, of course it was, everyone said it would be. I missed alcohol, everyone said I would and of course I did.

I couldn't be around alcohol, see it or smell it. I felt and looked better and I coped better. MN was thrilled, our relationship changed completely and overnight, I mean literally on every level it was better. I started to become the mum I wanted to be for Christopher and he started to trust my promises.

Sounds wonderful, doesn't it? The only problem was that not one time in those nine weeks did it feel real.

I was relying on willpower and shame. It was worse than coming off heroin. I didn't have any physical withdrawal symptoms, – by that time I had settled for a steady quarter bottle of neat vodka a night, with the occasional lapse if I was out with friends; vodka, no tonic, no orange, straight up and bloody lovely. I still thought I needed the vodka to help me relax and destress, even though there was no stress other than the ones caused by my drinking. But the psychological withdrawal was horrendous. Now I would be out in a supermarket, walking up and down the drink aisles in tears at the total war that was going on inside me. The raging arguments for buying alcohol were so much louder and more powerful than the ones saying "NO".

I would think of Christopher, conjure up his young face and see him nervously approaching me to ask a simple question, unsure of which mum would answer, and then see his whole body relax when I smiled at him and sat down to properly engage. This is who he had now. This is who he wanted and deserved. What the fuck was this screaming voice inside my head doing to him? What was I doing to him. Sonia STOP!

For the nine weeks I didn't drink, six of them were relatively easy. I was on a roll, relieved and happy and hoping that the sense of it not lasting, of not being real, would pass. That I would get used to this new, shiny normal and that I was done with drink. The last three weeks were hell. I was emotionally exhausted. I knew it was coming to an end, I knew I couldn't win the internal war., I knew I couldn't tell anyone, not AA and absolutely not MN; I was failing and I knew that to.

There was no incident contrived by me to justify my buying alcohol again, or even into drinking it. I didn't engineer an argument to absolve myself of the choice I made, or to blame anyone else. Nothing. I just couldn't fight it.

I bought the vodka and sat at home; I took the first swig straight from the bottle and started to weep. There was no golden trickle and warm glow, instead as I felt it travel through my veins, I knew I had just drunk poison. A poison that I was now certain I could never give up. A poison that was going to take my child's love and trust from me, and that ultimately was going to take my life.

I think that evening was the worst of my existence, nothing touched it. Not my mother's death, my illness, nothing. To know that I would spend the rest of my life lying to my son, unable to do the one thing he wanted, really wanted from me, and the only thing that he has asked me to do, "Please Mummy, don't drink", and I was not going to be able to do it.

And so a new life began, a new normal, a life I hated, a life in which I despised myself every day. I would buy vodka when Christopher was at school and MN working. I found all sorts of strange and unusual places to hide it. I didn't want to tell my son he couldn't go into my bedroom or that anywhere in the house was off limits, so I bought wicker storage boxes with lids and put them in various rooms. I would fill them with newspapers and magazines I had collected, under the pretense of 'keeping them to read later' and put vodka bottles in the middle. No one would be interested in these magazines so they wouldn't be touched. I never put the bottles at the bottom, in case the boxes were moved and the bottles clinked and gave my sordid secret away.

Empty bottles would be stored in the bed linen drawers underneath my bed, wrapped in towels to avoid detection by any noise. I would wait until I had a clear evening or day, then wrap the empties up in newspaper, put in a carrier bag and drive out of the area to a recycling centre and chuck the whole lot in. I had three or four different locations as I didn't want to be a regular at any bottle bank. I would drive past bins outside village shops and dump my carrier bags in there as well, literally anywhere that I wouldn't be recognised. On the odd occasion that I would be stopped outside a shop by a school mother, I would simply say they were leftovers from a party that I had forgotten to place with the recycling, but honestly, they were so well wrapped that no-one would have known there were bottles in the bags anyway.

Vodka at home would be decanted into innocuous, bottles of something that Christopher didn't like, so that he wouldn't either drink them or be suspicious. I found a place at the top of one of my kitchen cupboards where I kept the coffee he was too young to drink, and hid a disguised bottle up there. I would be preparing dinner and swigging away, sometimes bothering to hide the fake drink, if he came into chat, but mostly not. I didn't need to, and he didn't know, did he?

If occasionally I overstepped the boundaries I had put in place to deceive him about my drinking, and then woke up the next morning feeling unwell., I would put my 'illness' down to something I had eaten; which was stupid as four others had probably eaten the same thing.

My patience and tolerance towards Christopher and MN lowered without me realizing it. I became snappy and impatient again. The shame and disappointment in myself robbed me of the right to enjoy life, and it started to rob them of theirs too. As soon as I became aware of the change in me, I would sometimes catch myself in the moment:, maybe see the look of hurt and confusion on their faces, particularly Christopher's, and, with a huge effort reign myself in. I would apologise, make up some excuse for my behaviour, and pretend to move on. I became an expert in deceiving myself that they were unaware of the changes in me.

Worse still, I saved up my most 'normal' behaviour for the world outside. The effort and energy I expended on convincing unimportant people that I was fine, should only have been directed at those who loved and needed me. After a performance of appearing normal to the rest of the world, I would be exhausted and even more snappy at home. I knew I was Christopher's world; his only parent. I knew I was supposed to be his rock, and no-one else's. To this day I cannot explain what on earth I was thinking.

Bit by bit of course, MN realized what was happening. I think to start with this special man, who loved me so much, didn't want to believe it. But of course, no matter what lies I told, the evidence just kept piling up. He didn't confront me, he tried to understand, but no-one can understand if they haven't been a drug addict or alcoholic, even now that I am easily sober, I don't understand. As I wrote before, it was like an incomprehensible form of madness for which there appeared to be no cure.

I now think that I was at rock bottom. I had almost, but not quite completely, an insight in to my addiction,. I saw all the damage clearly and in technicolour. I saw the slump in Christopher's shoulders, I felt his silence as his distrust in his unreliable mother grew. He could tell me something in absolute confidence when I was sober and then hear me repeat it to someone when I drunk-dialled a friend. Actually, that only happened once, but it was such a serious betrayal by his mother and I can still see it in his face, in my mind's eye, right now as I am typing. For years he didn't trust me and even today, he says, "This is just between you and me, isn't it Mum?" but he knows now, even as he says it, that it is. That I would no more cut my arm off than repeat a word he says.

MN despaired too. Whilst I wasn't roaring drunk every night, I kept more of a distance to protect him once I had started drinking, and his hurt was obvious. I saw it all. We didn't really talk about it now, not unless I had one of my ugly outbursts. My lovely man just accepted it and let me be. It was that or lose me. They both deserved so much better.

Chapter 12: Today's the Day (or Maybe Tomorrow)

I had to do something. I had to change, but how? I thought by reading about the devastating consequences of my actions I would be able to shock myself into action. I started by researching alcoholism, the effects it has on the body and brain, and to read real-life stories of people who have overcome it. I was desperate to find the answer, a miracle.

I was still attending AA meetings intermittently but they just didn't seem to resonate with me. I listened and understood everything that was said. I got the process in theory, but not in practice. I was constantly hearing that being sober was a battle for life, that most of us would relapse at least once. I was terrified and I knew I had no fight in me. By now I was completely demoralized and drinking every night. Worse still, and I don't know why, I started to drink more. I would now buy a half bottle of vodka most days and, although I would rarely drink the whole amount in one evening, I would definitely be drinking more than half of it.

Over time, my mask of sobriety slipped completely. It slid drunkenly down my face and I was exposed in all my grotesque, alcoholic glory. I was still going through a version of normality, but I don't believe now that either Christopher or MN were under any illusions.

Every day I would wake up and say to myself, "This is it, this is the day. Tonight I will not drink". It was easy to say this in the mornings when I woke up feeling totally wretched and desperate. I would be lying in bed and check my phone first thing to see who I had drunk-dialled the night before. The anxiety attached to picking up my mobile, going through the outgoing calls, finding one and then looking to see the duration of that call was unbelievable.

If there was one, it could easily have lasted twenty minutes and I wouldn't have had a clue what the conversation had been about. Had I exposed myself as a drunk? Had I repeated a confidence, had an argument, insulted or offended a loved one? Should I ring back and apologise? What if I had said something totally stupid and possibly a lie? What if they called me back to discuss what I didn't even remember?

Oh God! And if there wasn't a call, I would have a few minutes reprieve before I remembered the house phone and rush downstairs to go through the same tortured performance. This was my shameful start of almost every day now, so it was easy to make those early morning grand resolutions that enough was enough.

As the day wore on though, the feelings of shame would diminish and I would start to review my decision not to drink that night. I would begin to rationalize that it wasn't that bad, that I had overreacted and I shouldn't be so hard on myself. I was definitely going to stop, I had all the information; I knew I had to, just not today, and so the farce would start all over again.

Christopher would come home, have his dinner and maybe if I was lucky, share something about his day. A very edited version I am sure, to keep it quick and over with as soon as possible, and we would settle down for the evening. I was still helping with his homework, still engaged in school, but in a much more brittle way. By brittle I mean that it was now emotionally and psychologically difficult for me to bend, be flexible. Any perceived slight would have me snapping aggressively.

Desperation to hide my alcoholism made it more obvious. I am naturally a free wheeler; easy come, easy go type of person, and I don't sweat the small stuff. Now there was no small stuff. Every innocuous question on any subject was viewed as a challenge to my integrity, my honesty, my ability to cope, my mothering. It was a gauntlet thrown down and I would fight until death to protect my 'honour'.

Back to our evenings, once we were settled, I would suddenly remember that something was missing, eggs, bread or milk for the morning. I would jump up with an "I must pop out and get…" and be gone. I would get into the car and drive to the shops and buy vodka, sometimes even forgetting to buy the missing item, or not having taken enough money with me for both and of course vodka always came first in any shopping trip.

To avoid being regularly associated with buying booze, I would drive to different shops in a five mile radius. I would always be crying as I drove, begging myself not to do it, but I just couldn't stop. I remember being in one shop, weeping as I asked for the vodka and having to explain that a close friend had died as the shop keeper was so concerned about my appearance. Then back home, decant the vodka and down my poison.

One night, probably to show me without saying that he knew, Christopher took the vodka out of the shopping bag before I got a chance, decanted it into the bottle I was using to disguise it and put in the cupboard, before he turned and walked out of the kitchen. I wanted to die with shame and remorse. I ran after him to apologise and make more empty promises. He shrugged his shoulders and said, "It's okay Mum, I know you are ill" My lovely boy was now making excuses for his wreck of a mother. The only parent he had.

As a teenager, Christopher wanted to go out at night and a new challenge hit me. How could I get around my drinking and be sober to drive him and pick him up? Drinking and driving, thank God, was never going to happen. So again, I worked around it. Sometimes now I didn't have my first drink until 11.30pm after I had picked him up and brought him home. I didn't like unexpected trips out because, as I wouldn't drink and drive, I would have to send a taxi at huge expense when necessary, and then worry until he was home. Still, not drinking was just not an option.

He began to ask me to leave when his friends came around. He would get up and leave whatever room they were in when I walked through. He would tell me to "Shut up" if I tried to speak to them for any length of time, and they would look at him in shock. He was so loyal to me that he would rather look rude in their eyes than expose me, but at the same time, he wasn't going to be embarrassed by me either. I loved to sing around the house, but he asked me to stop, he said it made him anxious. He would hear me purging in self-pity and self-disgust and leave me a drink of water outside the bathroom. He now never asked me if I was unwell, he didn't need to. He knew his mother was drunk.

Insight, into my alcoholism finally became searingly, almost blindingly, bright and clear. There were no longer any shadows for me to rest or recuperate in before I started again., it had become totally exposed to me. I went to the doctor in desperation again. and this time I was told quite clearly that if I didn't stop drinking I would die. My liver enzymes were too high and I was hitting danger point. Still, I felt completely helpless. I didn't want to die, I wanted to be sober so much that it haunted my thoughts constantly.

I do not think at that time that there was a single minute, of any day, when I did not almost pray that there might be a way to stop drinking. I asked myself over and over, "If knowing this doesn't stop you, what will?" But it didn't, nothing could. As a pathetic rear-guard action, I started to take vitamins and herbal remedies to support my liver function, and I studied nutrition to give my body the best chance of minimizing the damage I was causing all by drinking my daily poison, vodka.

I have never felt so powerless in my life. I started to realize that my death could only be a release for Christopher. He would be in pain for a while, of course he would, he loved me, but he deserved so much better than I could ever be. I was ruining his life, I knew it and I just couldn't stop. Every day now I was on the computer for hours scouring through all the tried and tested solutions to alcoholism as well as the weird and wacky, but there was none out there for me.

Chapter 13: Choices

At 50 years old, I had spent almost half my life as a drunk. At times a functioning one, at others a hopelessly non-functioning one. A tragedy of a woman who had everything going for her; a perfectly imperfect son, a lovely man, a home, friends who loved me and family.

The search for answers to my alcoholism became perfunctory and without any real hope, but still for at least an hour every day, I sat at my computer looking for an external solution to an internal problem. Still thinking that alcohol had chosen me, that I was a victim of an illness, I'd convinced myself beyond any shadow of a doubt that this was my life and my death, and that I had no choice.

I started to keep a journal. I don't know why. I think it was a love letter to my son. I wanted to write to him so that he knew how much I loved him. I suppose it was intended as some sort of apology, that maybe, one day, he might understand and then might be able to forgive me in the future. A journal that would tell him in the clearest possible way that he was the best, the very best thing that I had had in my life. My greatest blessing and that I was so sorry if he hadn't felt that way. If I hadn't made him feel that way. A journal that he could read after I was gone.

It wasn't possible for me to offer any sort of explanation that would make any sense, I didn't have one. How can you say you love someone more than life itself, and know that they depended and needed that love for them to thrive, only to then deliberately and systematically destroy your own life? And by doing so, know that you are also destroying a large part of theirs. That your leaving them will cause a mountain of unnecessary suffering from which you know they will never really recover.

By drinking myself to death, I would have tainted every aspect of his life. His confidence, self-esteem, and the future relationships with everyone he came into close contact with, that he should value and want to trust. With the lovely woman he deserved to have as a wife, with his children who he probably wouldn't have trusted me to be left alone with, and maybe even his career choices.

What could he have thought about my choice to put drink before him? What did that say about my love for him? What did that say to him about him? Was his happiness, his place in my life, and therefore in anyone's else's life so unimportant, so cheap that it came second to a £6 bottle of vodka?

I needed him to know that alcoholism wasn't my choice; I hated alcohol, even as I was pouring it down my throat. I hated what it had done to him, to me, to us. I wanted him to know that had there been any other choice I would have made it, not even just for him, but for me too. I knew we both deserved better. All this I wrote down., it all just flowed out of me. I would stop, re-read and write some more. As I wrote, sometimes crying as I saw my words appear on the computer screen, a strange understanding seemed to creep over me. The wheels of cognition started to slowly turn. I kept re-reading the word choice, 'not my choice', 'it had chosen me', 'I didn't have a choice 'and 'I wouldn't have chosen drink'. It all seemed to come down to one word, CHOICE. I started to question what exactly choice meant, and got this definition from a dictionary

Choice is "an act of selecting or making a decision when faced with two or more possibilities." It could be the choice between good and evil, and one option was an alternative possible course of action. 'You have no other choice.'

'Choice', such a small word, but with such a huge meaning.

I suddenly felt a door in my mind open that I didn't even know existed, that had been hidden and firmly sealed shut, suddenly groan as it slowly, almost imperceptibly, opened, allowing the tiniest chink of bright light to seep through. I am not into any form of spiritualism, but when I saw this glimmer of light, I knew I wanted that door open, and that the bright light might just lead back to the real me. The whole me.

This was incredible. I started to think, by the very fact that I had said to myself for so many years, I had no choice, meant that there *was* another choice, as that is what choice is. How could alcohol, a drink, a mere liquid, with no capacity for decision making, have made any choices for me? How could it have chosen me? That's wasn't possible!

I started to laugh at the absurdity of my thought process and then my second miracle started to happen. Alcohol, lost a miniscule amount of its power, and its space in my brain. I knew it immediately. I felt it. I didn't dare believe it of course, I didn't think this could be real. I thought I was just having a better day, or even just a better half hour, but still I felt its monstrous and all-consuming power diminish over me very, very slightly.

Now, that to you might sound crazy, so I need to explain a little of what makes the real me tick.

I have brought Christopher up with my strong beliefs and values, even whilst I have not lived by them myself. I know now that was always part of the reason I felt so much self-disgust. I always knew I wasn't real, but I didn't know why and therefore couldn't change; I didn't know what I needed to change. It was so much more fundamental than just stopping drinking. Anyway, notwithstanding my addiction, these beliefs and values are at the very core of who I am.

One of my most fundamental beliefs is, that whilst we are not responsible for all the situations we find ourselves in; we are, as adults, responsible for our reactions. We are responsible for the choices we make, and the actions that follow them. Once we take responsibility for our choices and actions, it removes the ability to blame others and ultimately allows us to move forward. Doesn't this sound incredible to you considering how I have written about my addiction? That alcohol had chosen me. and that I was a victim of alcohol. The disconnect between what I have always absolutely believed to be true in life and how I had been living was wider and deeper than the Grand Canyon, and I just hadn't seen it!

I have always told Christopher that taking responsibility for your actions and reactions leaves you firmly in control. If you are unable to say about anyone or anything, 'he made me do it', then you are not allowing 'he' to take any control of you or your decisions. I believe that is a very liberating way to think.

I have also always disliked and never understood 'victimhood' for exactly the same reason. Yes, terrible things happen, things that shouldn't happen, but on the whole (and obviously there are huge, shattering, life changing exceptions), being a victim stops you from moving forward in life and stops you growing. For me, it stunts you as you have abdicated responsibility for your decisions by choosing to be a victim. Again that little word; choice, choosing.

I sound much harder than I am here, I am not a judgemental person and I don't apply my beliefs or standards to anyone else, just to myself, and Christopher is the same.

Neither of us makes assumptions about others. As I said earlier in this book, we can never really know why a person does what they do, we don't know their history or their thought process and we don't know what it is they want to achieve by their actions. Sometimes the result of their actions is not what they wanted for themselves! We also know not to judge a person on one behaviour. I feel particularly strongly about this. A person who is bereaved for instance or going through a breakup and is hurt and angry, can act in a way they would never normally do. Do we then judge that person on how they acted during the worst time of their lives, when they are lost, confused, afraid or totally out of their comfort zone? I don't think so.

However, we also believe that whilst you don't judge anyone on one behaviour, if your actions have had a negative effect on others, you have a responsibility to then behave differently, to do something else, as it is important to acknowledge any pain or hurt you have caused. To us 'sorry' is not simply an easily said word, it is a change of behaviour, it is an action.

This is a snapshot of the real me, the way I have always felt and the way I am able to live now. Can you imagine the relief?

So, there I sat staring at the dictionary; choice. My choice... My choices... There is always more than one. I went downstairs and got my half bottle of vodka from the cupboard and put it on the side. There was a couple of inches left at the bottom.

As I looked at it a realization swept over me, an enormous mental tidal wave. Terrifyingly powerful, it crashed through my brain, my whole being, flooding my senses, washing my mind clean, ripping apart my thoughts and assumptions about alcohol, about the victimhood I had chosen to feel in order to justify my drinking. All my long-held convictions were battered in its storm, then as it receded, leaving me gasping in shock, it left the huge monster I had created for myself, the one I had allowed to dominate almost 27 years of my life, like driftwood broken, utterly smashed and washed up on a beach.

The bottle that stood before me was harmless, the clear liquid had no magic power, it wasn't calling to me, it couldn't. This liquid couldn't make me happier or more relaxed. It couldn't protect me or take away the pain. The bottle and its contents were not the problem, I was. I was not a victim of alcohol. Alcohol hadn't chosen me, I had chosen it. Now I was going to make a different choice.

I put the bottle away and went back to my computer in a daze.

I knew I wasn't going to drink again. I must have sat there for at least an hour, prodding at my brain, searching for the thoughts that had tormented me for over half my life. I tried to conjure up the feelings of desperation I felt around alcohol, the reliance, the fear of it not being there, the conviction that I couldn't cope without it. They were gone. Gone!

I was ecstatic for all of five minutes before reality kicked in. Okay, I had been here before, I had lasted nine weeks without alcohol and then gone back to it devastated by my failure. This was going to be the same but then I thought, 'have I really been here before?' During those nine weeks, I had been firmly entrenched in my self-constructed alcohol myths that it was more powerful than I was, that it gave me something rather than taking everything, that I needed, that something, even though it was the last thing I wanted. I had been afraid of a life without drink and so I had missed alcohol, couldn't be around it and hoped and prayed that my abstaining would last. This time it was different, I felt it in every part of me. I didn't want to drink, I wasn't going to drink. I was sober.

Christopher came home from school and in exuberant puppy mode I ran to tell him, to hug him and say, "It's over, it's gone, I'm never going to drink again".

He shrugged his shoulders and said, "I don't believe you".

I looked at him and the next thing I said changed our relationship forever, "I know love, I don't blame you. I have let you down so many times. You are entitled not to trust me. The onus is not on you to believe me, the onus is on me to prove to you that I have changed, and I will".

I think it was then at that moment, we both believed me, although he was absolutely correct to hold back. In the past if he had said he didn't believe me, I would have jumped at him, upset and demanding to know why. I would have been angry and used it ultimately as an excuse to drink again. I would have acted that way because, even though I desperately didn't want to drink, I had no faith that it would last. It would be just another futile experiment, the like of which he had seen far too many times in his young life.

Of course he didn't believe me. My reaction though surprised us both and he did hug me.

Chapter 14: The Beginning of Me

I didn't mention my not drinking again to Christopher. The poor guy was sick to his heart with hearing about alcohol, with worrying about alcohol, with the uncertainty of my moods. Elated one minute, running down the stairs with the next miracle cure I had read about, depressed and disappointed the next time when it didn't work for me. He needed alcohol out of his life in every way. It wasn't enough to not see the damn stuff in the house, he needed a break from wondering if I had been drinking when he came home, when or where I was drinking it. He didn't need to hear of my latest attempt to stop, how well I was doing or my struggles. He needed a total alcohol blackout. I knew all this instinctively and let the subject drop completely.

With MN it was different. I told him that I had stopped drinking, and what had happened. MN is an academic so it was easier to explain, but still of course he had reservations. Too kind to tell me of his doubts or to burst my bubble, he asked lots of questions and was supportive, but of course he too was wary. There are only so many times you can promise something and then break that promise before you are not believed and again, I understood that too and let it drop.

For the first time in over 20 years I had a sense of true release. I had peace where there had been turmoil, stress, anxiety, guilt, shame, self-disgust and self-pity. I stopped purging. I didn't need to anymore. The exhausting, emotionally debilitating internal tug of war was gone. Again, I was sober.

I continued to write down how I was feeling to work through any kinks I had in my thinking. I wanted to truly understand what had happened to me so that I could replicate it if I started to waiver. I didn't believe for one minute it would be necessary, but it was writing my journal to Christopher that had given me my blinding insight and I needed to process it completely. Honestly, it felt like a religious conversion (don't worry though, it wasn't!).

I had long understood that there are two aspects to addiction and that to successfully overcome any addiction, both must be addressed. First there is the physical addiction, the one where your body and brain craves whatever the drug is. The one that makes you shake and sweat through withdrawals, and I did feel anxious and shaky. I knew that the symptoms of physical withdrawal can last up to seven days and I did have some poor, sweat drenched sleepless nights, but whilst I was drinking almost every day, the amount I was consuming was not enough to trigger the serious symptoms that would have required medical supervision. I knew that but MN was not convinced so he was keeping a close eye on me. I also knew that once my system was free of alcohol and that my body and brain had chemically readjusted and rebalanced, that these physical symptoms would pass. I didn't feel in any danger at any time.

Then, there is the true monster of addiction, the psychological. This is the one that has the real power. The one that robs you of rational thought and overwhelms your every action. The one that only sees the drug, the one that demands the drug regardless of the trail of devastation it leaves in its wake. So, whilst I had achieved insight into my addiction, in what felt like years before I had stopped, and I knew exactly from the tone of my son's voice, his posture, his silence, and his sadness what my drinking had done to him, and still, because of the psychological monster, I had created, I could not stop.

I understood that my subconscious mind had, at some point, latched onto the fact that alcohol had saved me from pain, and that fact had remained locked there even when this was no longer the case. Alcohol had now become the cause of my pain, of the pain of everyone I loved, and yet my powerful subconscious still directed me towards it.

Our subconscious is incredible. It is responsible for over 95% of our actions. It is a computer that stores all of our memories; the ones we consciously remember and the ones we think we have forgotten. Its prime role is to protect us from pain and danger. A child who has been bitten by a dog in its very early years may well have forgotten the bite on a conscious level, but on a subconscious level, it has been recorded and processed so that the child goes on to develop a fear of dogs. All because the subconscious sends a warning when a dog approaches.

The same had applied to me. I believe that my tipping point into alcoholism was around the time of my mother's death. Drinking after her death had offered me a way out from the pain. It had blocked it, quite literally numbed it. My world had changed in an instant, not just because of her death, but because of the realization that everything I had thought and felt about her was wrong.

I now know that I was hanging by a thread at that time. Drink had stopped me from having to confront not only the pain of her loss, but also the pain of our smashed relationship too. Then as life went on, each time I needed to make a difficult decision, or found myself in a situation I couldn't deal with or didn't want to deal with, my subconscious remembered the relief alcohol had given me and offered it up as the solution. My subconscious was fulfilling its prime function, it had found a way to protect me.

Later, when I understood the devastation that my drinking had caused my son, myself and my life and I had been desperate to stop. When I had become so ill, when my son had begged me and as the agony of my alcoholism grew day by day,. my subconscious had the answer, its defence mechanism kicked in and offered me the only pain relief it knew, drink. On a conscious level, I had fought it as though my life depended upon it, which at the end it did, and still my subconscious had won out every time. It literally had no other option but alcohol to offer me.

I remember standing in the alcohol aisles of supermarkets and reaching my hand out to pick up a bottle whilst consciously begging myself not to do it, then being overwhelmed by a feeling that I had no control over my own limb. Crying and desperate to walk out of the aisle, or even the shop, but finding myself rooted to the spot, sometimes in front of a drink I didn't even like. The pull was that powerful. On occasions Christopher was standing with me saying, "Mummy don't cry", his sweet, young voice ripping me apart.

Even when I did manage to walk away, always aiming for the toy aisles to take his mind off the trauma, I would be compelled to sneak back as though on some destructive automatic pilot. I would grab a bottle, sometimes just the closest one and hide it in the bottom of my basket. The more pain I was in, the harder my subconscious worked to protect me by directing me back towards alcohol.

When I finally stopped drinking, I had no idea where this miraculous and incredible mental shift had come from. However, I grew to realize that I had come to understand something completely on a new level that the real me identified with immediately, and that offered my subconscious as an alternative.

Because of my core beliefs on choice, responsibility and victimhood, the ones I had brought Christopher up to believe in, the ones that are woven into both of our very beings, that are so fundamental to the person I am, this new clarity made absolute sense. I had given my subconscious an alternative, a stronger option completely in line with the person I am. Now when pain kicked in, alcohol wasn't offered to me, CHOICE was, "What will you do in this situation Sonia? How will you cope?" My choice, my decision, it was just up to me to make the best one. What did I want? Who did I want to be? What do I need to do to get to where I want to be? Then make that choice! It was like finding one of the missing pieces of a jigsaw puzzle, the jigsaw puzzle of me.

With that one piece in place, I was already less broken, the divide between my behaviour and my inner self was shrinking rapidly and my wholeness could move forward. I wasn't there yet, but I knew I would be. I kept repeating to myself, my drinking was my choice and my responsibility. I was not a victim of alcoholism, there was no external blame, it was just me.

I got it and I could deal with it, I could deal with me. Positive choices lead to more positive choices, strength to more strength and so the same with self-esteem, self-respect, everything I wanted I knew I could be. I just had to make the best choices. I was finally entering my internal comfort zone. I was no longer standing outside in the rain, wringing my hands in despair, searching for a door that had been so elusive for most of my life. I was now in a space I could work in, that I understood, that was real.

My choice not to drink had literally not one single downside. I was more interesting not less, I was more engaged not less, I was happier, not less, and I was more peaceful, not less. The 'not lesses' are endless. I am still the first one up to dance and the last one to sit down, I am just not embarrassing myself or being an embarrassment to others by shambolically stumbling around at the end of the night either hyperactive or in tears. As I started to question myself as to why I drank, and what it gave me, one question led to another and so onto a huge internal dialogue of one, me. No arguments, no screaming voices, no whispering voices, simply questions and answers. It was all within me, I just hadn't known it.

Over the next few weeks, I didn't mention alcohol to either Christopher or MN. Every day I got up and stood in front of my bathroom mirror, without a headache or remorse, but with gratitude for being sober. I would stare into my clear, unanxious eyes, I fell in love with my eyes, brightly sparkling and without guilt or pain. I would wrap my arms around myself and say out loud, "You don't drink anymore. I love you. I am so proud of you". I had never said I love you to myself before and I have never been proud without reservation either. I would even lean forward and kiss my face in the mirror. I had no fear for my future, for the first time in my life I trusted myself and I trusted my ability to be sober.

Both Christopher and MN could see the difference, but understandably they didn't trust me yet. MN in particular could see a fundamental shift within me. I was no longer brittle and nervy, the way I had been previously when I went through periods of abstinence. They had been unaware that during my earlier attempts to stop drinking, I had known that the whole time I was standing on a precipice, flailing wildly as I teetered, knowing that at some point in the very near future booze would come roaring back into my life and I would execute a spectacularly ungraceful swallow dive back into the abyss of alcoholism. I knew this would happen because drink had chosen me, and I knew I had no choice in the matter. Again, that word, choice.

I didn't overthink the change, I didn't want to. I just accepted it, accepted me and focused on moving forward. Focussing was a new thing for me, before my focus had been on drinking; the logistics of buying, hiding and drinking it and then on denying I had done any of these things.

Now, there was an enormous free space in my mind, and my life, I could focus on other things. My son had me 100%, the business I had created and then writing this book. I suddenly looked around me with new eyes. I noticed things when I was out in the evenings, different things other than the alcohol on the table and where and how much of it would be mine. I really looked at the people I was talking to, I engaged with them instead of hiding me from them. I started to laugh until I cried again. I have always loved to laugh and I think I am very funny (not a view shared by everyone, but hey ho, this book is about me not them), but I honestly though, I couldn't remember the last time I had enjoyed a deep, cleansing, belly laugh without the underlying anxiety that someone like me shouldn't be enjoying life.

Everything was new. All my experiences, both good and bad were heightened, all my sensations enhanced. For so long I had numbed myself from life, had abdicated all my feelings to drink and now a good day was amazing, happy and joyful. Simple things became a source of enormous pleasure; a walk on a sunny day, Christopher and I in the kitchen trying out new recipes, dropping bits of food on the floor and then hysterically scrambling over each other trying to grab food before Bandit wolfed it down. Laughing with MN, hugging friends, listening to any problems they might have, giving good advice, helping people. It feels so good to contribute, to be the giver not the taker. None of this had been possible when I was drinking, there was always the underlying shame or apprehension of the evening to come. Now I was no longer haunted by alcohol. I was no longer haunted by me.

Of course, the bad days came too, in many different forms. Stupid arguments happened because I discovered that I didn't seem to have much of a filter on my mouth. Stuff just seemed to come out, and of course with a reputation for being drunk, comments I'd make harmlessly now were occasionally taken badly because in the past they would have been meant badly.

Mostly though there was nothing upsetting. Maybe I was a little more honest, and if I did make mistakes, they were innocently made and in response to questions asked in social environments. I do remember people looking a little shocked at some of my answers, in particular a woman asking me if I liked her dress, and did I think it suited her, and I replied simply, "No", where in the past I would have been constructive. However, I was calm and peaceful so I rarely caused much offense and if I did, I would genuinely apologise and I became a source of fun (so much better than a source of embarrassment!)

To start with I felt a little shaky in situations around alcohol, not because I craved it, I didn't, but the terrain had changed and I had to learn to live in this new exposed environment. I think to start with I was a little quieter and shyer, as I gave myself time to establish a new equilibrium, to find a place in situations that worked for me. Still I learned quickly and kept mentally hugging myself with pride and love, and no matter what the situation, never once did my subconscious send alcohol to me as a solution. It sent me, the 'real me' that I knew had always existed.

I am a natural roll with the punches type of person. My non-judgemental attitude and resilience came into its own. Every time a situation arose that I had not dealt with before, and there were many, I stopped, and allowed myself to feel the normal, natural feelings associated with the situation. I would breathe deeply, have a good cry if necessary, look at myself in the mirror I kept in my bag now all the time and tell myself, "You're fine Sonia. This is a normal part of life, you will get through it, I love you", and I did. I knew and accepted 100% that I was the problem not the alcohol and that I was the answer.

Chapter 15: Understanding Me

Christopher was grudgingly starting to take notice of the change in me, but still not daring to believe in me. Why should he? I understood completely his reservations and just let him be. One day though, when he came home I happened to be walking past the front door and the look on his face stopped me in my tracks. All I could see in his eyes was anxiety. I was shocked and asked what was wrong, he quickly smoothed any expression from his face and said, "Nothing".

At the time, I was confused but later that night it hit me. He came home like that every day. That look was always there, he just hadn't expected to see me immediately. This is how he felt when he first saw me; anxious, and I hadn't seen it before, I had been too busy looking in at myself. I was drenched in shame and guilt. I abandoned my policy of waiting for him to come to me and sat down with him to chat.

I asked him what he thought when he came home, and again he replied "Nothing". I couldn't let it pass for his sake. After probably six weeks of being easily sober (and there was a big difference from the temporary 'don't hold your breath type sober' he had seen before), I held his hand and talked to him. I talked him through how I had become sober, what I felt now and the way forward. He got it immediately, I could feel it in him, as in the very best of ways, we are almost one. I told him that I understood he didn't trust me and that I didn't deserve his trust but that he would come to trust me.

My lovely young man was almost in tears he wanted so much to believe me. We hugged and with my arms around him, settled down to watch one of his favourite comedy shows, which made us both laugh at its ridiculousness. I felt him relax into my embrace, and knew that he knew, but that he needed more time.

I decided to attend AA meetings again. I didn't think I needed them, but I thought it would be good to put in place extra support should I wobble. I knew myself well enough to know this was no honeymoon period, but I also thought it would reassure Christopher and MN of my commitment to being sober, for them to see a willingness on my part to reach out to the accepted interventions.

I understood almost immediately why AA didn't work for me, or me for it. As before, I sat and listened to the speaker, introduced myself and proudly announced my 6 weeks of sobriety and engaged with the group discussion. The problem for me though was that the focus remained solely on when the last drink was, the terrible times and how difficult it was to stay sober. How many of us would relapse before we got sober, if we ever did. How important it was to reach out for help and support and that I would need to follow a structure for the rest of my life to keep me sober. I am not for one minute saying I disagree with any of the AA principles or methods, but I am saying, resoundingly, that I wasn't the right fit.

Alcoholism, like any illness or addiction, and its recovery, is not a one size fits all deal. There are certain behaviours that all alcoholics will recognize. We all act in pretty much the same way at certain times. We are all in denial, we are all ashamed, we all lie, we all hide our drinking, mostly we all hide our booze in similar places, but not in all aspects are we the same. We are as individual as people as non-addicts, and AA for me, did not seem to consider the person, which it would naturally be hard to do considering the size of the organization, what it does focus on is the alcoholic, on the one behaviour that becomes all our behaviour.

It deals with controlling the illness rather than curing it, in fact it supposes that there is no cure, it is an illness for life. I can't work like that, I don't accept that alcohol was the problem. The problem was my choice to drink it. If I continued to blame the alcohol

I was already in deep trouble. I had to accept that the problem was me, and that I was only going to be sober by dealing with me, by making peace first with me and then with others. You cannot help anyone else until you have helped yourself, if you do, you are working from a weakened state, where it is easy to trip and fall backwards. Only from a place of inner strength can you truly help and support others, make amends and move forwards.

I wasn't prepared or able to think one sober day at a time. To me, that was saying that alcohol would be in my thoughts every single day and that every single day would be a potential struggle for the rest of my life. This sounds exhausting and stressful.

Still, it would not be true to say that I never think about alcohol, I do, a great deal in fact, but I think about it objectively, as in how did it have that hold over me as well as trying to understand why I was so convinced that I needed to drink, when clearly, I didn't. But to be haunted by the spectre of it daily? To be afraid that if I am not vigilant my alcoholism will creep back into my life, again? I can't live like that.

I didn't want to count the days since my last drink. I don't know the exact date when I actually stopped, I only know the day Christopher told me he believed me, which was over four months later. I do know around the date I stopped, because it was between two birthdays in May; at one birthday party I was drunk and at the other I was sober, but the date? No, I don't know.

I needed to take full responsibility for both my drinking and my recovery. I knew that by handing over responsibility, on any level to any support or intervention, I was underplaying my only real ace in keeping me sober, me. I knew that by abdicating responsibility for my drinking, I was also taking away my responsibility to change. I had to remove any excuses, such as maybe, missing a meeting, having a bad day, or feeling unsupported, any excuse I could come up with.

I had to accept that there was no reason on earth that could justify my drinking again and the only way I could do that was by accepting completely that I, and I alone was responsible for my choices and reactions to any situation. As I said before, this way of thinking is totally in line with my core beliefs, and so is the way I work most effectively as a person.

Other support groups and counselling have also not worked for me because not only do I not want to look back and talk about my drinking; selfishly, I don't want to hear about other addicts' stories, struggles or progress either. There seemed to be so much fear of both relapse, and how to cope in a sober world. I am tired of fear, of being afraid, of carrying the huge dead weight of my alcoholism draped across my back, bending my spine until it feels as though it will break. I am bone tired of lying and hiding my drinking. I wanted to put it in the past where it belonged, acknowledged and being worked on by me, but not to revisit it every week. I want, and I need, only to move forward.

External affirmations that I am in control, that I am doing well, have very little long-term influence. I understand that the only affirmations that make any difference to my sobriety come from within me. No external intervention or person could get me sober, and no external support would keep me sober. I am so proud of my sobriety and I need to own it entirely. In the same way, I don't attribute any blame for my drinking, I don't put my sobriety down to anyone else either. If I do, then I am setting myself up for failure. I would be allowing myself an excuse and someone else to blame. I want no excuses. I am to blame.

I wish that all the marvellous interventions had made a difference, because if they had I would have stopped drinking the very first time Christopher begged me to. If I couldn't get sober for him, no group or therapy was going to keep me there. I know and understand now absolutely that only I can do that. And again, that's what works for me.

Sometimes I have conversations with MN where he asks me what role did he play in my becoming sober. I tell him in all honesty, that he had none. This upsets him and I try to explain, it's like a child who has an addiction; no matter what the parents do, how much they plead, how desperate they become and how much pain the child sees them in, it makes literally no difference. It's not that the child doesn't love the parents or wants to cause them the worry or pain, it is the last thing they want to do.

I know from my own experience that it was totally soul destroying every day to know that I was letting Christopher down. I cannot remember the last time during my drinking that I was not crying hopelessly every day. It is simply that, until the child makes the decision THEMSELVES to change, nothing and no-one can do it for them. Yes, the after care and support can be vital, but that shift can only come from within and it can be very hard to find. It is so easy to get stuck in a way of thinking that keeps you in the hell of addiction. I know this and am filled with gratitude every day that I finally understood not just my addiction, but me. Then the way forward was, and still is, easy.

I have never diminished the extent of the damage my drinking has done. I know exactly what I was like, who I let down, who I hurt and I know I cannot change a single thing. There is no magic clock that I can rewind and be the me I am now. I never try to place a more favourable spin on my addiction from my place of sobriety, there is no 'it wasn't that bad darling', to my son, or 'that's not the way it was, your memory is wrong'.

I can only apologise sincerely, give those that need it the opportunity to tell me how they feel, to relieve themselves of the burden of my drinking, and to consistently do something different and behave differently. I feel the doing something different is crucial to all those who have been affected. It is what they need to see from me most, and it is what I need to do most for me. And that is exactly what I do every day. Every time I flex my sober muscle, I not only regain a little bit more of their trust in me, but also the conviction that I have made the right choice. The stronger that muscle becomes, the more I continue to grow into a person I love and who gives love.

Ultimately, I have found that I can easily live a life that is real to me and that I have to deal with my alcoholism my way. A way that is supported by my own beliefs of responsibility, accountability and choice. I worked this out quickly and whilst I did continue to attend AA for a time, and the members of the group I attended were lovely, it really had no impact and so I stopped.

Chapter 16: Doing Something Different

The weeks went by and I was miraculously, easily sober. I had believed it from that magenta moment in my kitchen, when I had realized that I had chosen alcohol, not that alcohol had chosen me.

Still I had thought that I would feel a sense of loss, as though a treasured, long term friend had left me. Albeit one who had ultimately betrayed me, as my drinking had long ceased failed to live up to its early promise of pleasure and fun, and yet still one who I had known and understood for so many years that I couldn't let go of. I thought I might feel helpless and unsure in ordinary everyday situations, purely because I hadn't lived a normal life for so long, but none of those things happened.

Instead I felt unshackled and released from the drink-soaked prison that I had built for myself. That cold and dark place of addiction and self-loathing that I had been convinced I was sentenced to die in. Now I was soaring high and free, laughing out loud at my absurd mistakes. There were no wobbles, I had no alcohol cravings, no wistful thoughts, of 'I wish I could drink again', or 'life will be so dull now without alcohol' or wondering if I would ever be able to drink again, but this time in a controlled manner. Now there was nothing. Instead, and for the first time in my adult life, I felt I was someone worthwhile. Now I would have found it harder to drink than to not.

It started to become obvious to everyone that there had been a seismic shift within me; I was less frantic, happier and more at peace, they just didn't know what had caused it. I still didn't really talk about my non-drinking. I didn't want to know what anyone else thought about it, or to see the looks of, 'we hope so, but won't hold our breathes' on their faces, understandable as that would have been. I continued hugging myself every day and going through my morning ritual of staring into the mirror, and saying out loud, "I love you, I am so proud of you". It was a wonderful feeling.

As I gained in emotional strength, I cast around for something tangible that I could do to channel my new-found confidence, interest and joy in being alive. Something that I could create of my own, that I could be proud of. Something that Christopher could see for himself and point to his friends with pride saying, "That's my Mum, she did this all on her own".

But what to do? With no qualifications or work history that I could use as a stepping stone, my options would have felt limited to the drunk me hoping to get sober, now though, I felt that the whole world was opening up. The incredible feelings of liberation I'd had when I made that choice to stop pouring poison down my throat are still with me to this day.

Anyway, MN came into his own again, an outside the box thinker who had been wealthy, then broke then wealthy again. He had never really been employable and I liked and understood his way of thinking. I didn't want a job or to work for anyone else, I wanted my own business and he knew I could do it. We laughed, imagine me, an alcoholic to entrepreneur! That was my goal and I was going to do it.

Even though I had stopped drinking, I knew I had to limit, and hopefully reverse, some of the damage of my long-term alcohol abuse, so I started taking a keen interest in my food and nutrition. When I had thought it impossible to stop alcohol, I had started to study and read everything available on food, and its health benefits – probably even looking for a miracle in what I ate – another indication of how desperate I was. I would add anything to my life rather than take away the one thing that was killing me, booze. It seems so simple now.

I began to put into practice my knowledge of nutrition to kick start a whole mind, body rejuvenation, and the change was incredible. Within days of making small, consistent nutritional changes I was looking and feeling better than I had ever done before. My sleep, concentration, skin, hair, literally everything about me improved dramatically, I lost a stone in three weeks, and I had found a passion that I could build on to create something of value to myself and to others.

With my new venture in mind, I set about creating the environment I needed, both to work on my idea and to show Christopher that I was serious about being sober, motivated and in control; that I was doing the one thing that would prove his trust in me would be justified, I was doing something different.

We have a small bedroom to the left of his which was perfect as a little office. I threw out the bed and set my computer up on a tiny desk by the door facing the wall. I could easily have set it to face the window which would have given me a view of the garden, but then he wouldn't have seen me every morning when he got up. He has to turn to the right when he leaves his room, and walk past my closed bedroom door to get to the bathroom.

I wondered what he must have thought in my drinking days. Probably something along the lines of 'oh God, what's she going to be like this morning?' Poor guy. I would be either putting on my brittle, nervy 'great day' face in the mornings, which he knew was a mask, or be utterly miserable depending on my hangover (and they were definitely getting worse).

Now I wanted him to see me up, engaged in life, sitting at my desk, sans my 'morning after head' and working, and he did. Every single morning. I would be up at five-thirty in the morning, make my tea and be beavering away either studying for my nutrition exams or writing blogs and ideas for my website, and he could see this when he got up at 6.30am. Sometimes I did oversleep, but even on those mornings the moment I heard him stir I was up like a rocket and sitting at my desk before he left his room. Regardless of how the day started, I was busy, absorbed and I loved it. Not only that, but I found I was good at it too!

Our new morning routine was that when he emerged bleary eyed and tousled hair looking like the little boy he no longer was, he was met with a genuinely happy, "Morning darling, did you sleep well?" Obviously, he was shocked to start with, it was such a change. Christopher is not a natural morning person, and I am not sure how thrilled he was to be greeted by his mum in 'exuberant puppy mode', but still, I think it made him happy.

Gradually, he started to come into my tiny office and show an interest in what I was doing, so I put two small second-hand armchairs in, facing each other and a little table between the two. I would spread out my designs for my website, thoughts for logos and we started to plan how to create a business. Wow, we were doing something constructive together! I could have kissed him every time he sat with me on those mornings, but I didn't. I wanted this to be our new normal. For him to know that this was not another half-hearted attempt to do something new, that I wouldn't abandon it in the way he had seen me do so many times before with my attempts at sobriety.

Over the weeks, as his confidence in me grew, Christopher wanted to be involved. This presented me with the perfect opportunity to allow him to shine, to show off in front of his mum and he was brilliant. Firstly, he wrote me a 'mind map' – what on earth is that? Then after long chats about the direction I wanted to go in, he chose the company name, YOUtrition, which is both perfect and inspired as I wanted a weight loss and nutrition practice tailored to the individual, to 'you'.

I was delighted with his contributions because they were spot on for what I wanted to achieve. We both felt another huge shift happening. A shift that drew us closer, binding us tighter together as time went by with the powerful ropes of trust and mutual respect. We were building something special, not just a business, and we knew it. He saw me daily happy, positive and working hard on my studies and planning. I never mentioned alcohol and he didn't smell or see any physical or emotional signs of the hated booze.

Four months after I stopped drinking he came into my office one morning and sat down behind me. I had laid out some thoughts on flyers on the table and asked him his opinion, I wanted to know if he felt there was too much information on them. He picked one up, read it and said, "No, they're great, and by the way Mum, I believe you".

I half-turned around in my chair, preoccupied, to look at him and replied, "Good love, what about?"

His answer is the proudest moment of my life and I treasure it (I also bore anyone with it who will listen), because he said, "I believe that you don't drink anymore. I love you Mum".

I could have leapt from my chair screaming with joy; he believed me. He *believed* me! I wanted to run at him and hug and kiss him, but to be honest he already looked scared enough by my reaction before I had even moved. I think my face must have contorted into a mix of delight, gratitude, triumph, pain and tears. I picked up a flyer to compose myself and simply said, "Thank you. I love you too", and left it at that. I had done it, I was now a mother my boy could be proud of.

Our evenings had also settled into a new routine. He came home from school relaxed and chatty. Often we cooked together creating new recipes. Some were inspired, and some, with much laughter, went straight into the bin. If he was home, we would watch some TV together, or just sit and chat. If he went out, I was always ready, no matter what the time, to leap in the car and pick him and his friends up, and a couple of times from what felt like, the middle of nowhere at two-thirty in the morning! I could be relied upon in every situation because I was sober.

Since I was used to having a glass in my hand at night, I bought a beautiful bone china teapot and cup. In the winter months, my evening drink consists of lemon and ginger herbal tea and during the summer slimline tonic. If I was home late after a day in London, I would phone Christopher and saying, "Make me a drink, I'll be home in five minutes" and either the tea or tonic would be waiting for me. Alcohol now simply did not exist in our lives. There was no stress, strain, anger or lies. I didn't want it, I didn't miss it, it was gone.

Chapter 17: What Sonia did Next

Whilst I continued to study for formal nutrition qualifications, Christopher provided herbal tea and encouragement. I got excellent marks in my exams and we both celebrated me with my new tipple of slimline tonic water with ice, lemon and lime. Him with a cold beer. My certificates started to come through and I framed them.

A friend wrote up my website and helped with the final design, also the printing of my business cards and flyers, and Christopher started distributing them. In one week, my amazing son had delivered 3000 door-to-door solely by himself. I know how proud and happy we both were because we kept telling each other.

He would come to me if I was working late in my office and ask me to stop and come and watch some TV with him, to share an article or podcast he had seen that might be of interest to me, or to share a funny clip he had found on YouTube. I never made much of these interruptions, but I was aware of them every time he sought me out, wanting my company, and I think I probably must have been glowing with love, pride and gratitude for our new relationship, our new normal.

MN remained amazingly supportive and interested, but on the whole, I kept our creation, YOUtrition between Christopher and myself. MN understood perfectly and never interfered. He knew of my need to show my son something different, he knew that the business I was building was part of my apology. The biggest part, the part Christopher would understand and believe, the 'doing something different' part.

Within the first year of being sober I had set up my new business, YOUtrition. I had chosen a hugely saturated market with its diets, diet clubs, weight loss lotions, potions and gels everywhere. I was unfazed by this as I wanted to do something different. To offer a new perspective, one I knew from my long and painful experience with addiction actually worked when restriction, deprivation or new eating plans won't.

From the time I truly wanted to stop drinking, a good 15 years before I actually did it, I knew what I needed to do. I needed to not buy the bottle of booze, not open the damn thing, not to put it to my lips (let's just bypass the glass), and not to drink it. I knew this and I couldn't stop. And then I could, just like that.

I could because I *thought* differently. I stopped attaching feelings and excuses to a liquid. I stopped handing over responsibility for my feelings and my life to a drink, a drink I then blamed for my unhappiness. I stopped expecting something that I was swallowing to make me feel better, bring me comfort or security, or to make my day brighter, take away my pain, make me more confident, funnier and happier. I knew that no drink could make me anything more than I am, only less. Once I accepted that, not drinking was and is easy.

With YOUtrition I wanted to apply similar principles to food. Food is of course different, as we have to have a relationship with it in a way that we don't with alcohol. Alcohol we can avoid and put out of our lives, this is of course impossible with food.

Food is a necessity of life. Eating together can be a time of bonding, a way of nurturing. Preparing food can be an expression of love and care, as well as a source of nourishment and the road to good physical and mental health. However, it is only when it is *real food* that is eaten, not food products, and even then it is eaten for the right reason, hunger. When it is eaten for almost any other reason, and when we chose food products, not food, then weight and health issues arise.

I challenge my clients about their food choices and reasons for eating. I ask questions that only they can answer and together we find alternative ways of thinking around food. Habits that are learned can be unlearned, new tastes developed, new thoughts around food.

One of my early clients said to me, "I had such a bad day that I went home and ate a whole packet of biscuits", my response to that was,

"Well done, you have an excellent way of dealing with your bad day! That packet of biscuits must have made your day so much better".

Of course her answer was a resounding "NO".

Through talking together, she realized that she had in fact compounded her bad day with making a choice that had made her feel worse, both mentally and physically, and the end result was that she was filled with self-disgust.

No-one deserves to feel the way I did when I was drinking; powerless, helpless, despairing and out of control, and yet far too many people feel exactly the same way around food. Without realizing it, they have given food power over them and have become stuck in that way of thinking.

I wanted to use my experience to help them see this basic fact and then how to reframe their thoughts on food. To understand their history with food, their early relationships with it; were they given food as a reward, or as comfort. Were they forced to eat foods they didn't like or maybe denied it as a punishment, or through poverty. My aim was to move them forward, to unstick them from their old thoughts and feelings, the same ones that I used to have around alcohol, and in the same way that I became sober, I knew I could help them achieve the weight, health and body they deserved.

Put food, like drink, in its rightful place, as a source of nourishment, and you take away its power. Then you can really enjoy all its wonderful tastes and textures, its sociability, its bringing together of family and friends, as well as occasional treats and all without guilt. Expect it to fill any void, other than the one in your stomach created by physical hunger, and ill health, weight gain and disappointment in yourself are the inevitable depressing, unhappy consequences. I can't live like that, and I want to help others to stop like that too.

So, this is exactly what I created YOUtrition to address. Lovely, easy recipes are not enough. Yes, I offer those, along with the planning strategies that make weight loss much less daunting, but until you address the *why* of what we do in any aspect of in our lives, no long term, sustainable changes can be made and this is my absolute passion and area of expertise.

Slowly I started to get clients. I did all the social media, which Christopher had to help me with as I was clueless. I wrote programmes, weight loss plans and started to run weekly weight loss classes. I wanted to get my clients to the point of making excellent food decisions and to think differently for themselves, because they deserved it. I wanted to help them leave all their accumulated food baggage, built up over years of conditioning behind them, to cut out the food stress and replace it with healthier, happier habits where food was a source of joy, not a stick to beat themselves with.

I was determined not to be another weight loss club that clients could simply abdicate their responsibility to by returning week after week, month after month and year after year to stay on track. If they kept coming back to me, I had failed them.

The amount of work involved was enormous. I wrote everything from scratch, and put my all into everything I did. As well as my programmes and plans, I wrote a Food Diary to keep in their handbags; a great motivational tool. I want to understand how my clients live, and to identify areas of food stress, so that I can really make a difference. I care passionately about all my clients and it shows. I don't offer gimmicks, or fads or sell any weight loss products, I simply offer excellent nutritional advice along with my unique perspective.

I 'got' my clients and they 'got' YOUtrition. They loved the support, the recipes and the planning. I make sure that every client gets exactly the individual support needed.

My dream of using my experience to help others was working and my business was growing.

I had proved I could do something different and so another piece of my jigsaw puzzle fell into place.

Chapter 18: Loss

As life moved on in its sober new course, my relationships with everyone important to me improved, and all as a direct result of the improvements I had made in my relationship with myself.

I was honest with anyone who asked about my drinking now, and I think that most of those who asked were shocked by the extent of it. I am shocked now when I look back. I also know that those of my friends who had experience of alcoholism, really struggled to equate my new-found sobriety and the difference in my personality, with the alcoholic struggles of their own loved ones, and occasionally there were a few unpleasant conversations. With their own experiences in mind, they would become upset and tell me it wouldn't last, and that I wouldn't, or couldn't stay sober.

These outbursts never affected me, for two reasons. The first was because the person was not actually upset with me. Yes, their anger was directed towards me, but as an outlet, and I quickly understood that it was their pain that they were showing. Their anguish over the alcoholic in their life who had hurt them, or someone close to them. I recognised their weariness over the lies and broken promises and their sadness and despair that he/she couldn't/wouldn't stop. They wanted to know why I knew I would stay sober, why I was different, why I was special. They wanted to tell me that I wasn't either of those things, that once an alcoholic always an alcoholic and that one day I would 'fall off the wagon'.

I have never felt special or different just grateful; unbelievably, eternally grateful that I was able to have that magic moment of understanding. I know how rare those moments can be. I also know that when that moment of understanding came, I grabbed at it, held it tight and trusted myself not to fail me. I know I could easily have ignored that moment, or made excuses the next time a tough situation came my way, but I understood the power of my choices and made the only one I could live with. I chose to be sober.

The second reason was that even those closest to me, don't really know me. Not their fault, how could they? They have only ever seen the drunk me, even when I was sober, for so many years. However, I do know me. I know my strengths and my weaknesses and I know how to deal with me, but not with alcohol. I know who I want to be as a person and I know that person is sober.

Those that told me it wouldn't last, didn't take into account the 'me'. They just saw the alcoholic, and believe me, with my subconscious on board, the sober me wins every time – in fact there is no battle, I just don't drink, there is no effort.

After 18 months of our miraculous new life, a sober, happy, peaceful one, Christopher finished school and wanted to spread his wings a little. I felt that he needed to be away from home and from me; our relationship was now strong. He trusted me, we were great friends, and I understood his need to be by himself. In my heart, I would have liked a few more years at home with him, with our new normal, but I had to support him and give him the room to grow away from me that he deserved. The fact that he now felt ready to go was also another indication of his trust in me, I don't think he could have articulated that, but I know it to be true. The anxiety from his eyes had completely gone and he no longer asked how I was feeling. He didn't need to, he consistently saw his real mother and he believed in me.

We decided that a college close by would be a good starting point. Just over an hour from home, it was easy to get to and from and so he enrolled in an Accounting course. We rented a small flat a ten minute walk from the college, which we decorated and he moved in; one very excited and happy young man. Christopher made friends and settled into the program, he found he was good at it and we spoke for five minutes almost every day. He got a job at a coffee shop at the weekends and took up boxing in the evenings. He was now living a life free of the stresses that I had heaped onto him for far too many years, and at last he was able to breathe.

Whilst it was wonderful to see him that way, I struggled with his leaving. I felt low, the house was too quiet, even with our little Bandit, who was such a comfort. There was no-one other than my little dog to greet me in the morning (Bandit now slept on my bed), and it brought back to me clearly all the years I had failed my lovely Christopher. I was very upset when I remembered his childhood, all that precious time I had wasted being a sad, hopeless drunk. In my mind, it became an even bigger problem than it had been, and that is really saying something!

Christopher was unaware of all of this. I was not so selfish as to burden him with my feelings. He was happy and so should I have been, but it was hard. Still, drink did not enter my mind. By now it was just not an option, neither consciously or subconsciously. I no longer viewed it in any other way, not even as poison.

About five weeks after Christopher left, Bandit became ill, his eating dropped off and he became listless. Initially I thought this was normal as he was becoming an elder statesman. He was almost 12 years old, but then he stopped eating completely and I took him to the vets. After some tests, I received the awful news that he had kidney failure and that there was nothing that could be done for him. Such a huge shock. I arranged for the vet to come to our home three days later; I had to have those last days with him. I brought Christopher home and we went for his favourite walks, he chased a few squirrels on his last outing out and we cuddled him at home at night. Neither Christopher or I wanted him to be at home when Bandit fell asleep, so I took my boy back to his flat the night before the vet was due.

On a Monday morning, with MN there to say goodbye, I held our littlest boy tight as a kind vet inserted a needle into his tiny leg and Bandit drifted off into his final sleep. He didn't fight it the way I knew some animals do, he just sighed and relaxed, he was ready to go. Our little Bandit left our lives the way he had come into them, in my arms, wrapped in a blanket and with a loving kiss. He was gone and we were no longer the Gang of Three. I was devastated, completely heartbroken and with no coping skills. I composed myself long enough to phone Christopher and tell him that Bandit had left us, and to reassure him that it was peaceful and loving, and then I fell apart.

Shortly after my telephone conversation with Christopher I suffered a huge panic attack, the first in many, many years. I felt it rise up and engulf me, crashing down and forcing me to the ground. I started crying hysterically, shaking and terrified. I wanted to scream and maybe I did, I don't remember. I know that all the guilt I was feeling about Christopher's childhood, the pain and damage I had caused, the missing him, the loss of Bandit, the loss of my mother, of Dave. It all seemed to simultaneously smash into my consciousness. There was too much loss and I was grief stricken again.

I must have lain on the floor for over an hour, crying constantly. I wanted everything back, and I wanted to do it all again but this time properly, Christopher's childhood, my childhood, my mother, Dave, Bandit. And I couldn't have any of it.

Eventually I roused myself and walked slowly into the kitchen. On the floor was Bandit's water and food bowl, with the pathetically small amount of breakfast that I had put out to tempt him. It was untouched, although he had sniffed around it that morning. I picked the bowls up and spilling both the food and water down my jumper, hugged them to my chest. MN walked in to comfort me; I went mad, shouting at him to get out, to leave me alone. My poor, gentle man backed out of the room looking shell shocked. I ran after him screaming instructions to burn Bandit's bed, and I threw the bowls at him and into the garden.

Slamming the door behind me and locking him out I sat on the sofa hugging Bandit's blanket, rocking backwards and forwards. I felt I was losing my mind again and there was a terrible feeling of desperate madness that lasted three days. Thankfully, knowing that we would be losing Bandit, I had arranged for one of Christopher's closest friends to stay with him for the week. I knew that with him there, I wouldn't hear from my son. I let myself go and tried to absorb and process the multitude of painful emotions that ebbed and flowed through me. One minute terrible pain, the next calm and then a panic attack. And still, not once, did alcohol come into my mind.

Good friends called me concerned but I wouldn't pick up their calls, I guess they must have spoken to MN for reassurance and got none. One just wouldn't give up, and turned up at my home. For God's sake, go away! I had to let the bloody woman in or else she'd be still banging on the door now.

She took one look at me and said, "Let's go to Devon". Knowing that this is one of my favourite places, one that Christopher and I had visited many times with Bandit for short holidays where we walked, ate cream teas and played with our littlest boy in the sea (and I of course drank), my friend thought it might help as clearly, I was sinking. Surprising myself, I agreed and we left the next morning for a three-day trip. It was perfect. I walked on the beach every morning for miles, crying and comforting myself. Later we would go out for a couple of hours exploring and then back for my evening walk on the beach whilst my lovely friend cooked dinner. It was peaceful, I grieved and I relaxed.

With dinner my friend drank wine, two bottles to be precise, each night. And each night I drank tonic water. There were no thoughts of alcohol even when it was right in front of me, when the easiest thing to do would have been to pick up the bottle with the excuse of, 'just the one, I need it right now, I'll stop again tomorrow'.

The bottle was right beside me on the dinner table, I would hardly have had to move my arm to reach it. It was open, I could smell the wine and my glass was next to it, but there was nothing. No pull, no 'shall I/shan't I?' moment. Why would there be? I knew that it couldn't offer me any comfort or support, it couldn't ease my pain. I wouldn't be able to forget those I'd lost, and I didn't want to anyway. I realized that by grieving I was honouring my loved ones. That by talking about them I was keeping them real and alive in the special, safe and tender place in my heart, where they belonged. Somewhere I could visit them in my dreams and remember them with the love and gratitude I felt for all they had been to me. I didn't want to forget anymore, to try to drown out the memories of my lost loves out with booze. They didn't deserve that and neither did I. I wanted to hear them again. Another piece of my jigsaw puzzle fell into place.

I understood even during the panic attacks, that the distress and grief I felt was the normal that everyone else goes through, I had just never experienced it before. Although on some level I was shocked by the intensity of it, I accepted that as well as it being a new emotional experience, there was also a huge backlog of grief which had come together in the tiny package of Bandit and his passing.

I knew it would pass when I was ready and that by allowing myself to go through this pain, without trying to avoid it or self-medicate it and myself into oblivion, I was giving myself the best possible chance to heal. I had to acknowledge, even if it was just to myself; my agony, my loss, my guilt, and I did. Together in Devon we watched silly movies, laughed at her drunken craziness and talked for hours. So, my friend drank her wine as I drank my slimline tonic and never once did I think there might be an alternative, another way of coping, a way out. There was just me and I would get through it. Again, I knew, that even then, in that dark hour, I was free.

On our return, the only person who didn't ask me if I had drunk any alcohol was Christopher. I understood completely the concern of MN and my friends, and it was wonderful to offer honest reassurance that not only had I not drunk anything, it hadn't even crossed my mind. I felt the general sigh of relief and was happy for them, they had suffered for far too many years worrying about me.

Christopher didn't need to ask. He knows and understands me far too well for good and for bad, and he knows that I am done with booze.

Chapter 19: Moving On

Although I continued to find life a little sadder and the days a little less bright, now that my home was empty, no Christopher and no Bandit, drink still didn't come into my mental line of vision.

My feelings were raw and it felt as though all my nerve endings were exposed now that the false alcohol drenched protective skin that I had coated my life against had been stripped away. Every physical and mental knock bruised my now tender emotional self as I struggled to regain the happy place I had been in, and the peace I had felt. MN was still kind, supportive and loving, YOUtrition was building slowly, and whilst I was still proud of it and myself, some of my joy had gone. I instinctively knew that there was nothing I could do other than be kind to myself and let a new, healthy and this time truly durable protective skin grow over.

I have never formally meditated, but I did start to examine my emotions more. I didn't panic when pain or upset came my way, regardless of the enormity of it. I wanted so much to feel alive, to be a part of life, to actually have a life instead of hiding from it, and I understood that pain was a natural element of that life. Without pain there can be no pleasure, and I had drunk my way through both. I was never truly happy during my drinking days. Even the sober ones, there was always the spectre of alcohol looming like the Grim Reaper, ready with his scythe to cut me down during the best of times. Just knowing that I would drink again, maybe not even that night, but that I would, was enough to dull the shiniest day.

Bandit's death had shown me that I needed to develop coping skills, I couldn't disappear to anywhere every time an emotional body blow floored me, and the only way we gain those skills is through experience. I had begun to believe that I was a naturally resilient person so I trusted myself and let go. I let my feelings in and I welcomed them both happy and sad.

I realized almost immediately that pain was not a monster to hide from like a terrified child. It was on a spectrum, both physically and mentally that goes from 1 – 10 (1 being a nagging feeling of discomfort to 10, an unbearable agony). Had I really needed to self-medicate from 1 upwards? Of course not. In fact I didn't need to self-medicate at 10 either. It had never made any pain go away, it had just stored it up for later, ready to explode shattering not just me, but everyone close by. The collateral damage of an alcoholic's behaviour can cover a very wide area!

I understood that pain can be viewed as either a reason to surrender and shy away from life, or my new choice, to learn from. It can make us more empathetic, kinder and less judgemental, as we can if we choose to allow ourselves, grow to understand why others might act in a certain way when they are hurt. For me it became a valuable learning curve, I am not sure I have ever hit that terrible 10, nor do I believe that at my worst I have inflicted that level either. Another incredible shift. The more pain I let in, the more I coped. The more I coped, the stronger I became and the more I grew into a person I valued. Plus, miracle of miracles, the stronger I became, the less pain I felt, even over my saddest losses.

On the flip side of that, the more happiness I was able to feel, and happiness for me is on the same 1 – 10 spectrum, (1 being content – 10, deliriously happy). Most days now I feel consistently a 7 – 8. I was becoming the balanced and flexible person I had only dreamed I could be. Another piece of my jigsaw puzzle fell in to place.

Finally, I allowed myself to grieve, for my mother, for Dave and Bandit, but most of all, I grieved for Christopher's childhood. I started to have flashbacks of incidents where I was dismissive, cold or angry and shouting at my little boy. The flashbacks around the time of my illness were the worst.

I wondered how he must have seen me, his mother, his supposed rock and safe place? What did

I look like to him through those trusting, beautiful blue child's eyes? How frightened he must have felt, how alone and uncomforted. The flashbacks came unbidden and at the strangest times. I would burst into tears, almost on the verge of a panic attack and would have to stop whatever I was doing. I couldn't control them. It was almost as though by allowing myself to feel pain, it had finally found an outlet and raced towards it in case I changed my mind. I had opened my personal Pandora's box and there was no shutting it. And still alcohol never entered my mind, not once, not for one second. Never.

I let it all out, and as it fell, I laid it out in front of me. I picked up and examined, piece by painful, tattered piece the evidence of the devastation my drinking had caused us, and knew for both his sake and mine that I had to deal with it.

Now sober for almost two years, it was time to talk to Christopher.

Chapter 20: Christopher

My relationship with my son was blossoming into the mother/son/friendship relationship he had always deserved, and I had always dreamed of. It was now wonderfully, mutually nourishing, loving and supportive. He trusted me with his secrets, not all of them I am sure, he is my son after all and there are some aspects of his life I would really rather prefer he kept between him and his friends. He has however, shared easily his hopes and dreams for his future, what makes him happy and sad, his interests, likes and dislikes. I am so proud to say that there is very little we don't discuss. I visited him most weekends if he wasn't working and we would talk for hours either walking, or over lunches out. But to start with, we didn't really talk about my alcoholism.

As I wrote earlier, my lovely son had had enough of hearing, seeing or thinking about alcohol where I was concerned. He didn't need any more drink crap in his life, so I never mentioned it, and nor did he. However, I was aware of a number of instances where it was obvious that it was on his mind, or rather instances where it was clear that he was so proud of our new normal. One time occurred when we were sitting in a pub garden having lunch. The waiter took our order and brought our drinks over. I ordered my usual slimline tonic with ice and lemon, and on that occasion Christopher had a bottle of lager. When the drinks came we were in the middle of a conversation, animated and laughing.

The waiter put the drinks down and, barely pausing I thanked him, picked my drink up and smelt it. "There's no alcohol in this is there?", I asked.

"No" came the reply, and Christopher and I continued our conversation, but then he reached over and held my hand for a brief moment with a look in his eyes and a flush to his cheeks that stopped me mid-sentence. Thankfully, I realized before I asked him what was wrong, that I had inadvertently acted in such a natural way, it had reinforced his belief in my sobriety.

Another time was when we were out shopping in our local supermarket. To find the product I needed, we had to walk past the aisles of alcohol, and in that supermarket, there are many of them. As we walked by them all chatting, I was oblivious of all the various bottles on display. Christopher however, wasn't. Again, I noticed a sidelong look in my direction and a flush to his cheeks. I am not sure if he was remembering past traumas in these aisles or just feeling pride and reassurance, but I suspect it was a little of both. As with the pub incident, neither of us mentioned the moment and today I hold those looks in my heart, cherished and with pride.

I knew that it was not enough that he believed me. The fact that our relationship had gone from strength to strength, did not in any way diminish our past. Or rather my past behaviour and I needed to understand his feelings, and so did he. It was imperative that the past was dealt with properly. I had to make sure his wounds were cleaned, if he was going to be able to move forward and become the contented, confident young adult, with the healthy self-esteem he deserved.

Whilst I knew that any wounds I had inflicted would heal over time, it was very important how they healed. If untended, they would leave angry, red, puckered and interwoven scars. Livid and oozing infected pain that could slowly travel through his body to his heart and from there pass right through to those who would be most important to him in the future, infecting his whole life. I knew this type of healing having experienced it after my mother's death, not just in me, but in my siblings too. However, if his wounds were gently cleaned, washed free from the specs of gritty pain, soothed with the ointment of understanding and covered with a sticking plaster of honesty and trust, there would still be scars, there couldn't not be, but those scars would have the best chance of feeling smoother to his emotional touch and with simple, straight, silvery lines, hopefully barely visible to the eyes of his psychological wellbeing.

I started to broach the subject and the first few times we both became upset. I was so scared of what he might say about how he had felt, of how I had let him down, of what he remembered that I could barely speak without bursting into selfish tears. And yet again, my behaviour determined his, and he too would be close to tears, but even then I could both see and feel his need to talk.

We got into the habit of walking whilst talking. The face to face over lunch or dinner chats were too hard. Walking by the river or in the woods was much easier, we could both turn away when necessary to compose ourselves, or say aloud something that was too hard to say looking directly at each other. So at times we did both get upset, but still as we walked the necessary conversations flowed.

Christopher started by telling me the feeling he remembered most and that was fear. Not fear that I might physically hurt him, thankfully he never had that, but fear of my reactions; fear of my unpredictability. Would I shout over harmless, innocent mistakes, dropped drinks or food, unimportant mess made? Was his room tidy enough? Would I mind of he had an accident trying to make me toast? Would I be angry or upset if he forgot to take his shoes off and left a muddy trail? I was utterly shocked. If someone had asked me what I thought the affects might have been, fear would never have been one of them.

He had been afraid to ask me for help or tell me something was wrong, because he knew if I was unhappy it was because of him. He had been afraid that if he couldn't make me happy I would leave him. Can you imagine how terrible it was to know that as a small child, my son, this lovely young man had feared his mother, his only parent?

My sole role as his mother was to be his protector and nurturer in life, to love and educate him, to ring fence him from pain, to keep him sheltered from monsters and storms. Only, in his young mind I was the monster and that he lived in the storm. He talked of feeling cherished and adored, but also of feeling lonely at times and tired. Weary of worrying about me, loving me and hating me at the same time. So often seeing his lovely mummy who could change her mood over nothing; of course though, it wasn't nothing that changed my mood, it was the very first drink that changed me, but he would have been too young to know that.

He remembered asking me, "Mummy, why have you changed?" and when he said that, I remembered too. He said he hadn't felt good enough – if he had been good enough I would have been happy. He had struggled to equate his two mummy's; the adoring one and the cold, and distant one. The funny, huggy laughing one, the mum who would have walked through fire for him and the one who would shrug away from his touch. The one who took on the school and fought for him all the way, yet sometimes couldn't be bothered to sit and watch his favourite TV show, preferring a sneaky drink. Worst of all, truly the worst part, was that he thought all of that, all the trauma, fear, unpredictability of mood and behaviour, was normal. He thought that was what childhood was. He wasn't angry, he said, "I didn't know any different did I, to me it was just normal".

We talked about his teenage years, he told me he couldn't understand why I didn't stop drinking when he asked me to, but that by then he knew I was ill. He also knew how hard I had tried, he said he could see it. He knew that I wanted to be different and he had many happy memories, but often there was an underlying worry that I would change suddenly, become morose or upset. He always knew immediately when I'd had a drink, even when I denied it completely.

His friends thought I was brilliant, but he deliberately kept my interactions with them short. The fun-loving craziness that they saw, he also saw, but knew it was shot through with anxiety which could make me unpredictable. He loved our walking holidays during the day but was never able to sleep well at night, no matter how tired he was for worrying I might wander onto the beach with a drink and fall asleep with tide coming in.

At home we were close, but if I had been out for the evening, he didn't lock his bedroom door, or even close it at times if he felt I had overdone the drink, in case I needed him in the night. What a mess I had made, what chaos and uncertainty I had caused! Of course it should have been my door unlocked, left ajar, in case he needed me after a night out, not the other way around.

I cried as he told me that he had always looked in on me first thing in the morning before school as I slept off the night before. Had always come in and kissed me before I awoke. He told me that he tried to put his arms around me even though he hated the smell of booze. He wanted so much for me to be well and I wasn't. He said he told me he loved me every morning, but that I just didn't hear it.

If I had not heard him before, I heard him then and I have never felt so much self-disgust as I did listening to him finally unburden himself. This time though, self-disgust did not turn into self-pity.

I wanted to tell him over and over how sorry I was, but if I had, I would have placed another equally heavy burden upon him. He would have felt compelled to make his tearful, hand wringing mother feel better. He would have had to say, "It's okay Mum, I forgive you" and I would have dried my tears, hugged him and felt better until the next wave of guilt hit me, and then repeated the same pattern of tears and begging for forgiveness. Where would that have left him? Still playing a role he should never have been cast in, in a drama that had no place in his life. I had cocked up both our lives, and I'll clear up the mess this time thank you. None of this was about me, nor about what I felt or thought, or even what had happened to me. This time it was all about him and what I could do to help him.

I had to make him understand that none of the turmoil I had created in our lives, my behaviour and unhappiness, was in anyway his responsibility or fault. I was totally to blame and he was totally blameless. I made it a priority to make sure that he knew this in every possible way; in every conversation and in all my actions. Slowly, he did understand. He obviously wanted to. I saw him absorb everything I said as I explained, or tried to, about what I was thinking when I drank.

I told Christopher that I now knew that my heavy social drinking had spiralled out of control after my mother's death. I hadn't realized this before I quit, but I believe now that is when my drinking slipped into alcoholism.

I told him that whilst I didn't know why, I had felt there had been no other outlet for me than alcohol, nothing else with which to ease the shock and try to hide my grief. There was no other relief, no support, in my mind, that could have made a difference. After that, I had become trapped in alcoholism, and ultimately I had believed what I'd heard and what I feel is the general understanding; that very few alcoholics ever recover from their addiction. Those who were lucky enough to escape, seemed to fight a war for the rest of their lives, always remembering the date of their last drink, being rightly proud of it, but still aware. That alcohol would remain in their lives like a feared spectre at every feast, following them; sometimes clearer in their vision, sometimes a grey wisp drifting by, but still always there. Forever.

I felt that maintaining their sobriety must have added an extra gruelling dimension to cope with in times of stress. An added, heavy layer to carry, to drag them down and impede their way forward. This extra burden seemed to me to make any tough time even tougher, as the one thing they had relied on to

197

take the edge off stress and anxiety, now had to be factored in as something to be avoided at all costs. I don't even know now where those thoughts came from, but I do know that I am not alone in thinking them.

I thought I would have to be heroically strong to take on that 'battle of the booze' let alone win it, and I knew that I couldn't spend my life fighting. I wasn't strong enough to stop, to meet life face-on and deal with it, but I was strong enough to carry on drinking in the full knowledge of all the damage I was doing!

I told him that I had been trapped in a way of thinking, created entirely by myself, that offered me no other alternatives. That I felt alcohol had chosen me and that I had no choice in the matter. That without consciously realizing it, I had become scared of life, and how to cope with it. I had spent so many years looking inside myself in shame and disgust, that I had lost sight of the fact that everyone else has pain in their lives, on some level at some time too, and most others were able to cope. Yes, sometimes we had seen friends go off the rails as they struggled during difficult times, but they had worked their way through it and come out the other side. Some had self-medicated for a period, and then got themselves back on track. Sometimes they remained shaky for a while, but still they knew that the alcohol route was not the answer. I however had decided to live my life off-piste, and I'd dragged him with me as we careened out of control through all of everyday life's usual small struggles, creating even bigger ones as I drank.

I had thought that I drank to relieve stress and pain. It was only after that miracle moment, in the kitchen, that I realized that all the stress and pain I was experiencing was caused by my drinking. That I was repeatedly doing the one thing that put us in such a sad, bad place over and over, and thinking that it was the cure, never the problem.

I told him it was all about me and how I had viewed myself and my place in a world that I had created, and the lack of my ability to live in that world; that it was nothing, absolutely nothing to do with him. That he was the bright, burning star in that unloving, dark world I had made for myself, and that I had loved him from the moment I had first seen his 'little purple cone head' (my brother's first word to describe him when he was born). The problem was though, that I hadn't loved me and that one fact had spread like stain into his life.

As we talked, over the months, my trusting, loving son would listen, his head on one side just as it had been when he was a little boy and I was teaching him to read. He would often change the subject for a while and then come back to it when he was ready. A couple of times he called me when I got home and we would talk for hours on the phone, sometimes him in tears and sometimes me, and as time went on both of us laughing until we cried. Happy and sad, they were all good, healthy, healing tears.

Everything sifted through his mind and gently landed in small, manageable, deposits that he could scoop up, examine and let run through his fingers to be disposed of wherever he felt was best and in his own time, and he did. I am always honest with him and he appreciates that, although I do have one caveat, and that is he must never be my counsellor, only my son. I don't know how many others would have understood me, but this boy of mine and my MN knew me, trusted my honesty and believed me.

As time passed, my self-disgust turned into something empowering, it turned into determination. Yes, I had messed up spectacularly, but no more. I knew that I had been given a second chance and there was no way I could have blown it, even if I had wanted to. My crutch of alcohol had been gone two years now, it had turned into dust that day in the kitchen and had long since been swept away with most of my other rubbish. Now I was my own crutch and his. A strong, but flexible one that we could both lean and rely on, regardless of what situations blew our way. There was no moving this one, crafted as it was from a place of inner strength, the understanding of myself and love for him. Another piece of my jigsaw puzzle fell into place.

I think over those many months we talked, I finally grew up. I also told him during our, sometimes painful, sometimes hilarious conversations about my life and experiences. I was unaware that I had never discussed any of these before. I wasn't trying to explain or justify myself, but I hoped that by sharing some of the milestones in my life and my reactions to them, he would be better able to understand some of the why's of my crazy behaviour. How successful a strategy that has been I am not sure, I do know that even to my own ears, I do at times sound completely mad.

One life experience he particularly laughed over when he heard it for the first time was that for a time, way back before he was born, instead of tea and toast for breakfast, I had often enjoyed a vodka and orange and a line of coke.

So, we were both happier, both of us clearer on the each other's feelings and motivations and whilst still a work in progress, I felt that by talking, we were truly moving forward, very slowly, and in Christopher's own time, putting the past to rest.

Chapter 21: Peace

With all the positives emerging, my home still had an emptiness to it which I continued to find hard, so we decided to get a new dog. This time a puppy. I had always taken in rescue dogs, apart from Bandit, who I had chosen for Christopher, and now we agreed that I should get one just for me. A puppy, a baby, to give me a happy new focus.

Together we found the ugliest little mug alive. Can't you just hear the adoration in these words? A gorgeous little piece of scruffiness with a huge underbite whom we called Gorby (MN's choice and contribution to the dog finding exercise). I drove four hours to get her, she threw up on me and I was sold. I brought her home and put her in her new bed. That was the only time she set a paw in it at night, and that was only for twenty minutes. Tired after my long drive home, I took this scared little pup, who was in a completely new environment and away from her mum for the first time, upstairs with me and we slept curled-up together on my bed. Or rather as it is now, our bed. Poor MN, side-lined again. I was in love.

Now the New Gang of Three, Christopher, Gorby and I, met up on the weekends he was free. If I arrived at his home while he was still at work, he would ask me to come and meet him in the coffee shop he worked in. At first I was unsure, he had never really wanted me around his friends before, but that had all changed and now he wanted to show me off. Sometimes he even put his arm around me! Can you imagine my pride?

Now as we walked, talked, enjoying each other's company and watching over our crazy Gorby, our conversations were normal and easy. They ranged from the sublime subjects to the ridiculous which would often reduce the both of us to tears of laughter.

He rarely asks me questions regarding drinking now, but he knows that if he does, I will answer them honestly. I am entirely responsible for my choices, I do not have the need to do anyone else down or to blame anyone, but still he asks me a lot of 'what if' questions. "What if my Dad hadn't abandoned me, would that have helped you cope?" and "what if your family had lived closer and you had told them you were ill, would it have made a difference?" There are so many 'what if's' and none of them will help him heal and go forward, which is all I want. I have no idea what, if any difference, they may have made anyway, so we don't dwell on them. I made my choices, no-one else. An invaluable life lesson for him too. Still though, my lovely

Christopher has often said to me "Mum, don't be so hard on yourself".

Often he sends me screenshots of the recovery statistics for alcoholics and drug addicts, depressing reading I must say. Always with these screen shots is a simple sentence, such as "I love you Mum", or "I'm proud of you Mum". Christopher has no doubts about me and nor do I.

Other comments he makes, that make me proud of myself, such as, "Look what you did Mum, you went from being really sick and unhappy to the best person I know, and you did that all by yourself". Or, "you're the biggest success I know" and "no one is stronger or more honest than you". Then there are the ones that take my breath away and make me so proud of him, "Who's to say I would have been a better person if you had been sober?" and, "who's to say I would have been nicer, kinder or less judgemental?" finally, "None of my friends are as close to their Mum's as I am to you" It is other remarks, such as "I like the person you made me. I could have turned out to be a nightmare even if you hadn't been drinking, but I didn't and it's all because of you" and on one occasion, coming up to Father's Day, "what shall we do on Father's Day?" I must have looked a bit perplexed at this one because he elaborated, "well, you've always been my Mum and

my Dad – a better Mum but still a not bad Dad!".
Never one to wax lyrical, these words mean
everything to me.

I am not trying to give the impression that all is
perfect now in our little world. It is good and we are
happy and strong, but I have no doubt that my
alcoholism will cast a long cold shadow over both of
our lives for many years to come, hopefully mine
more than his. I have no idea if the past will raise its
ugly head and bite him later in life, but I plan to be
there with him to deal with it if it does, and if for
some reason I cannot be, he can refer to this book
which I believe will help him.

I still struggle with the knowledge of the pain I
have caused and on some levels, I am glad of that. I
don't beat myself up, there is no point, but I do
utilize that knowledge positively, particularly with
Christopher and a lesser extent MN, as a powerful
motivation to be different. To acknowledge to them
without speaking the words, as they both ultimately
want to move on and have their well-deserved
peace, that I know, I understand, I am sorry and I
love them.

There was one more thing that I needed to do,
someone to visit and make peace with. My mother.
Twenty-five years after her death, I finally visited her
grave again with Christopher. We took a watering

can, flowers and some cloths and washed the headstone. One of my brothers, Mike, already tends to her grave when he visits from France every couple of months. It was Mike who had carved her headstone himself and put it in place with another of my brothers, Joe. Christopher and I sat by her grave, pulling out the few weeds left since Mike's last visit, and smoothing out the gravel.

We chatted for an hour and I told him about his grandmother. I told him she had found life too difficult with nine children, but that she had loved us, and that she would have adored him. I told him about her funeral, about his Uncles carrying her coffin to her grave, how cold the day had been and how there had been horses running in the next field. As we got up, I rubbed her gravestone, gave it a kiss and we left. Good bye Mum. I love you.

The last piece of my jigsaw puzzle dropped into place. A bit battered around the edges, with some of the colours worn off and an unidentifiable crazy mishmash of a picture that is definitely not to everyone's taste, it was complete. I am whole again.

Now after the 27 years of my life and the 16 years of his that I spent as an alcoholic, this is where I am today. Where we are. Christopher is busy at college and when he is home I can hear him shift in his restful, restorative sleep without the anxiety of wondering which mother he will wake up to. He loves helping me with my business, 'our business' he would say, because we are building it together. He practices recipes, and sends me ideas. I see clients and run my classes and write articles. My programs are popular and in demand, and I even have my own Health & Fitness show on local radio. I am considered a professional success.

On a personal level this is how my son now sees me, and how I see myself. I am a good, decent woman, kind and generous, great fun and a bit nutty. Someone to trust and rely on, whose word is her bond. A woman who works hard and enjoys life, who loves to be social, to sing and dance. Who is good in a crisis and a good friend in tough times. I am the mother her son deserves and can be proud of. Standing with him wherever he needs me most, beside him when he needs a friend, behind him to catch him if he falls and squarely in front of him when he needs protection and defending, and all because I had made a different choice, the choice to be sober.

At the beginning of this book, when I wrote that I thought I would be a drunk forever, lacking everything I valued in life, a tiny speck of me had always hoped and whispered from a secret place hidden deep within me, "This isn't me". It couldn't be, but still it was.

Now, at 53 years of age, with confidence and pride in the woman I am today and every day, a person of quality who deserves and has self-respect. A woman who has love and lives a truly worthwhile life, I write with the deepest of gratitude, THIS IS ME!

Printed in Great Britain
by Amazon